Praise for
Why Teams Don't Work

Winner

**Financial Times-Booz Allen & Hamilton Global
Business Book Award
Best Management Book, The Americas, 1995**

"*Why Teams Don't Work* is a great business book because it looks up from the bottom, not down from the top, as most do. They describe in winning terms the tensions and anxieties that keep organizations from achieving worthwhile goals."

Michael Treacy, co-author, *The Discipline of Market Leaders*

"We all want to be part of authentic teams. How do we go about it? Finley and Robbins set us on a compelling journey to teams success by helping us see and embrace the secrets we often hide from ourselves and our teammates."

Richard J. Leider, author of *The Power of Purpose and Repacking Your Bags*

"Michael Finley and Harvey Robbins, despite the title of their book, are the most pro-team guys you'll ever read. What they have done is to bring our consideration and discussion of teams out of the classrooms and board-rooms and into the trenches of the workday world. The message is that teams CAN work but just not in the way we may have been led to expect. Robbins and Finley not only set us straight on the real world of teams but also tell how to make them work for our organizations."

James A. Autry, author of *Confessions of an Accidental Businessman*

"Teams generally fail not because managers don't manage, but because there is something wrong with the mindset of the team. An entitlement atti-tude, secret agendas, glory-hogging, and hiding under the covers are sure ways to drag a team down. *Why Teams Don't Work* hits it on the head."

Judith M. Bardwick, author of *Danger in the Comfort Zone*

"This is an immensely helpful book. Finley and Robbins show that that the secret of great teams isn't found in buzzwords or gimmicks, but in bringing out the best in every individual. Their suggestions are compassionate, yet tough-minded and practical. Read this book, heed its wisdom, and experi-ence the simultaneous pleasure of feeling better about yourself and seeing your team's performance and productivity rise."

Robert K. Cooper, Ph.D., advisor to organizational leaders and best-selling author of *The Performance Edge* and *Executive EQ*

"This book is a masterpiece of explanatory journalism."

John Bicknell, *New Orleans Times Picayune*

"Too many books on teams focus on the how-to technicalities. It is rare to find a contribution where the personalities of the team members occupy central place. *Why Teams Don't Work,* an extremely enjoyable book, takes on this challenge, and by doing so provides a highly original view on team behavior."

Manfred Kets de Vries, Raoul de Vitry d'Avaucourt Professor of Human Resource Management. Professor of Leadership Development, INSEAD

"Robbins and Finley make a compelling case that the reason teams fall short is less a management issue than a failure of the soul of the team. This is a book about group intelligence, challenging us to understand one another in our rich human complexity . . . I like it a lot."

Danah Zohar, author of *Rewiring the Corporate Brain* and *SQ: Spiritual Intelligence*

"*Why Teams Don't Work* is that rarest of beasts: a book of truths. Using language that is remarkably entertaining, honest, and brief, Robbins and Finley dissect the hackneyed assumptions about teams to explain why so many companies that switched to teams 'have not been experiencing the organizational bliss they counted on.'"

Jim Kane, Linkage, Inc.

"Serves well any manager's interest in maximizing productivity and quality improvement with teams. Recommended for all quality professionals!"

Quality World

"With its slant on the psychological, this one's a gem."

Soundview Executive Summaries

"This book is for the millions of workers who either volunteered or were enlisted by a team, gave their honest best to the cause, and then wondered why."

Library Journal

"The title tells it all—if you believe in teams and want to make them work for your organization, this book is for you."

Pete Nelson, Thomson Learning

"For all public library business collections."

Library Journal

"Robbins and Finley are provocative writers . . . the read is fast, funny, and highly stimulating."

Business Book Review

"Reading *The Wisdom of Teams* without also reading *Why Teams Don't Work* is like making a peanut butter-and-jelly sandwich without bread. You may very well end up with a sticky mess! *Why Teams Don't Work* is a wonderful excursion through the minefield that threatens to destroy the best team intentions."

Dan R. Dick, Director of Quest Resources, General Board of Discipleship

The New
WHY TEAMS
DON'T WORK

The New

WHY TEAMS DON'T WORK

What Goes Wrong and How to Make it Right

Harvey A. Robbins
Michael Finley

BK

BERRETT-KOEHLER PUBLISHERS, INC.
San Francisco

Berrett-Koehler Publishers, Inc.
450 Sansome Street, Suite 1200
San Francisco, CA 94111-3320
Tel: (415) 288-0260   Fax: (415) 362-2512   www.bkconnection.com

Ordering Information

Quantity sales. Special discounts are available on quantity purchases by corporations, associations, and others. For details, contact the "Special Sales Department" at the Berrett-Koehler address above.

Individual sales. Berrett-Koehler publications are available through most bookstores. They can also be ordered direct from Berrett-Koehler:
Tel: (800) 929-2929; Fax: (802) 864-7626; www.bkconnection.com

Orders for college textbook/course adoption use. Please contact Berrett-Koehler: Tel: (800) 929-2929; Fax: (802) 864-7626.

Orders by U.S. trade bookstores and wholesalers. Please contact Publishers Group West, 1700 Fourth Street, Berkeley, CA 94710. Tel: (510) 528-1444; Fax: (510) 528-3444.

Printed in the United States of America

Printed on acid-free and recycled paper that is composed of 50% recovered fiber, including 10% post consumer waste.

Library of Congress Cataloging-in-Publication Data

Robbins, Harvey
    The new why teams don't work : what goes wrong and how to make it right / Harvey Robbins and Michael Finley.—[2nd ed.]
      p. cm.
    Rev. ed. of: Why teams don't work. c1995.
    Includes bibliographical references and index.
    ISBN 1-57675-110-4 (alk. paper)
      1. Teams in the workplace. 2. Teams in the workplace—United States. I. Finley, Michael, 1950– II. Robbins, Harvey. Why teams don't work. III. Title.

    HD66 .R583 2000
    658.4'02—dc21

                                    00-033687

First Edition
06 05 04 03 02 01 00   10 9 8 7 6 5 4 3 2 1

Interior Design: Gopa Design   Proofreader: Henrietta Bensussen
Editor: Elinor Lindheimer   Indexer: Paula C. Durbin-Westby
Production: Linda Jupiter, Jupiter Productions

We dedicate this edition to our wives
Nancy Robbins and Rachel Frazin, our real-life teammates.
For putting up with our occasional dysfunctionality
and, during the toughest times, mopping our fevered brows.
Good women and true, you are the best.

▼

Table of Contents

Preface

Why Teams Don't Work surprised us. When we created the first edition in 1995, we intended it as just another book on the teams bookshelf. After all, we were just a teams coach and a business reporter, toiling somewhere in the snowy Midwest. It wasn't logical that our book would be a hit. But, 50,000 copies and a *Financial Times* "Best Management Book of the Year" award and many hundreds of fan letters later, we are forced to conclude that we wrote a good book.

What's so good about it? A consultant with a top global firm collared us in the lobby of a London hotel with her theory.

"Teams have been imposed everywhere from the top down," she said. "You've got consultants selling teambuilding packages by the yard. You see executives bragging in magazines about their terrific team skills. Then there are organizational dynamics professors writing long dry papers with lots of boxes and arrows. But none of those people sound like they've ever actually been on a team, or know what it feels like when a team is struggling. You do. Your book," she concluded, "is the antidote to all the others."

We blushed. But it's true. We've had team leaders come up to us almost tearfully at conferences to thank us for the bottom-up approach, and our focus on team intelligence.

Team intelligence, the linchpin concept of this book, is not the team's IQ. (Though IQ comes in mighty handy on most teams, and lack of it has sunk many a team to the bottom of the sea.)

Team intelligence is intelligence about working together. A team that is smart about itself knows where its strengths and weaknesses are. Team members know what each of them wants and needs. They know about one another's peculiarities, and how to get the best from one another. And they know when to stop bugging one another. Intelligent teams have to fight to achieve this level of awareness, and they have to fight to keep it.

Most teams, we're sorry to say, come up short in the smart department. Some of this is the team's fault. Team members don't respect one another, they don't listen, they hide what they know from one another. They act as if they are not a team, and indeed, they are only a team in name, a group of people who hold meetings. These "teams" need to either get smart ASAP, or disband.

More often teams aren't smart because they are not set up to be smart. The organization they belong to doesn't provide them with goal clarity, or a sensible line of command, or the tools to do the job. The team is made to live in an atmosphere so toxic and so paranoid that you can't have a simple conversation, much less share ideas.

Poor team intelligence—about goals, about processes, about decision making, about individual team members' needs—is why teams don't work.

Which brings us to the title of the book. If we could correct one misconception about *Why Teams Don't Work,* it would be the inference people make, from the negative-sounding title, that we lack confidence in people's ability to work together.

In truth, we are passionate advocates for teams. We believe in people. We like people.

But we do get angry sometimes, and we do lose heart, and we do have negative thoughts when we see how brutally organizations treat teams, and how teams mistreat themselves. So often, this brutality arises not because anyone is mad at anyone else—it's just the way things are in the organization. No one wants it to be that way, but no one can make it stop. This is team unintelligence.

If this is an "anti" book, then it is anti-betrayal, anti-lying, and anti-stupidity. We'll accept that negativity. Why, we'll wear it on our lapel, like a white carnation.

Remedying these team failures is the reason we wrote this excellent book. We commend it to you to get the teams you are on to work together better, and provide greater satisfaction for everyone.

What's New

We're very pleased that *Why Teams Don't Work* has been through numerous printings and is now embarking on a second edition.

What's new in this edition? Lots. We've added 65 new pages, and torn out 28 old ones.

We focus everything through the lens of *team intelligence*—the smarts a team has to acquire together in order to perform. Team intelligence is a kind of play on words. On the one hand, it means good ideas about teams—the intent of this book. But it also refers to the intelligence successful teams must have, the knowledge their members have about one another, that is the key to high performance.

On balance, we can report that this edition is more *practical* for everyday use, while having a more radical flavor. We're madder than ever at bad bosses and toxic team members, so we load this edition up with hints on how to avoid the one and hang a bell on the other.

We add a section on *team leadership*—what special qualities and skill sets a leader has to cultivate in order to lead. Team leadership, it turns out, requires more than mere project management skills.

We talk more about the impact of *personality* on teams. Not just why Dave and Edna can't get along, but what Dave can do to work better with Edna, what kind of leader Dave would make, and how to get Edna to check her e-mail more than once a month.

We provide some nifty new concepts for addressing team problems. Like boundary management, to create clarity for so-called empowered teams. ("You are empowered to do whatever it takes to solve customer problems, provided it doesn't cost more than $100.") Or the "team of one" (end quarreling, miscommunication, and delays by eliminating everyone from the team but one).

We tie *technology* to team dysfunction. The Internet is creating new ways for teams to communicate. Some of this is great, but it poses problems for team members who aren't up to snuff technologically.

We update our *history of teams*. With the perspective of years, we can see now that teams were not just copied from Japan, or created as a consequence of downsizing. They represent a healthy new stage in the evolution of organizations, in which people's talents are finally more important than the hours they clock.

We unearth several *myths about teams* that really should have been in the first edition. Like, the notion that sports teams and your team have anything whatsoever in common.

But the biggest change is our *definition of teams*. The first edition looked solely at corporate teams, especially self-directed work teams. This edition takes a broader perspective, seeing teams and team problems everywhere—not just in large corporations, but in small firms, nonprofits, civic groups, schools. Teams aren't just "in" organizations anymore. Just as often, they straddle organizations, bringing representatives of different groups together to solve problems.

A team is just people doing something together. A team can be together for 20 years. Or a phone call lasting 20 seconds may bracket the creation of a team, the completion of a task, and the subsequent dissolution of the team.

That's the vision. Now here's the book.

Acknowledgments

First off we want to thank our excellent author's representative, Andrea Pedolsky of the Altair Literary Agency. Andrea has been working with us for many years now, originally as our editor before ascending to agentry. She's been a steady influence on our writing career—the sensible left-brain counterweight to our right-brain playfulness. Half of the things she does, we say, "Why didn't we think of that?" The other half, we wonder how she did it.

Harvey wants to thank all the teams he has ministered to at client sites in his 20 years as a teams trainer—at Honeywell, 3M, Toro Co., IDS, International Multifoods, the U.S. Treasury Department, Southern Companies, and elsewhere. The people he worked with are the heroes of this book, the team pioneers who taught us so much with the hard lessons they had to learn.

Mike wants to acknowledge the Masters Forum, the Twin Cities executive education program with which he has collaborated for the past decade, reporting on the trends and ideas bubbling up in the business realm. Much of the wisdom in this book consists of the parboiled and reconstituted thoughts of these fine teachers.

We also must thank Steven Piersanti, Jeevan Sivasubramaniam, and the rest of the team at Berrett-Koehler Publishers. Berrett-Koehler is something else, a publisher that still loves publishing. Better yet, it's a business publisher that gives a damn about the people side of business. Lucky us.

Harvey Robbins
Mike Finley
June 2000

part one

The Dream of Teams

▼

chapter one

The Team Ideal

A generation ago people didn't talk about teams. Oh, they existed, but they were conventional, function-bound things. There were accounting teams, finance teams, production teams, and advertising teams—all made of specialists in parallel functions or "silos." Everyone on a team did pretty much the same thing.

Functional teams spent a lot of time together, and spoke the same functional language. Not having to deal with one another's "differentness," functional teams had something of a free ride.

Wow, has a lot changed since then. The conventional silo team is still out there. But it has been crowded out by scores of other kinds of teams.

There are work teams in which everyone has the same skills, but each person is assigned a specific task. There are project teams, where people with different expertise each tackle a different part of the task. There are functional teams, and there are cross-functional teams.

There are interorganizational teams and intraorganizational teams. Some teams, like Army platoons, live and breathe together. Others join together across time zones, language differences, and boundaries. There are teams that work together for twenty years and those that team up for only a minute or two, then fade away.

There are leader-led teams and leader-less teams. There are teams in which everyone takes turns leading. And teams on which everyone is leading all the time.

There are teams of a hundred, teams of a dozen, teams of two—even teams of one (we'll explain that).

A Short History of Teams

Though teams may seem new, they aren't. We hunted and gathered in teams a hundred thousand years ago. Someone led, everyone did what he or she was best at, and shared in the outcome. By the time of Hammurabi, teams were already old hat. What we do today is only a modest variation on that. The team is the natural unit for small-scale human activity.

The catch is that word "small-scale." With the Industrial Revolution, which began in the 1700s and has taken the planet by storm, the common model for many businesses drastically changed. Mass assembly machinery and techniques developed in the early 1900s meant that a single man, woman, or even child in a factory could be ten times as productive as his or her cottage equivalent, working the old way.

The Industrial Age peaked with the development of scientific management. This theory, propounded by Frederick Taylor, an American, attempted to optimize the productivity of organizations by assigning specialized tasks to individuals. Bosses were bosses. Below them were ranks of managers. Below them were countless supervisors. And below them, at the bottom of the organizational pyramid, were the multitudes of rank-and-filers, each one assigned a single task, like tightening a screw or attaching a hose or stamping a document.

Scientific management yielded the phrase "a cog in the works." It was, in many ways, the wonder of the world. Henry Ford's River Rouge plant in Detroit was an impressive four-mile-long monument to scientific management. The United States government was also a form of scientific management. It broke a large organization down into a nearly infinite assortment of tasks or bureau drawers. The bureaucracy this created was very steep and very deep, from the clerk sorting applications in the U.S. Patent Office all the way up to the ultimate boss, the President of the United States.

Technology ratcheted the machine age even tighter with the development of commercial mainframe computers in the 1950s. Large companies were suddenly able to perform accounting chores, such as billing, buying, cataloging, and payroll, that were unthinkable even in the big-company boom of the 1920s.

Bolstered by mainframe computers, big companies became megacompanies. The emphasis began a subtle shift away from uneducated manufacturing crews toward well-educated professional functional groups—people skilled in engineering, finance, distribution, and even technology itself.

By the 1960s the idea of teams made of flexible, multifunctional members, especially in big companies, had become nearly extinct. Functional teams such as accounting teams, design teams, and information services teams existed, but specialization and separation was the typical pattern.

Then the American postwar prosperity bubble popped. Corporations had become so immense that they were out of touch with their customers, and charging too much for value delivered. Workers were not asked to contribute their knowledge to the task of increasing an organization's ability to compete or make a profit. A deep trench separated management from workers; management was the brains of an operation, and workers were the muscle, and that was all.

Labor relations became one of two things, each as bad as the other: adversarial to the point of intracompany war, or complacent to the point of indifference. The driving mission of adversarial industries like mining and oil seemed to be to keep workers down. The sloppy mission of complacent industries like autos and steel was to cut sweetheart deals with labor to mop up the gravy between them, and the hell with the customer. It was the age of bloat.

The rest of the world, ruined by World War II, was rapidly

rebuilt. Fiercely competitive Japan, Germany, and other countries, seeking an edge against the U.S., were experimenting with new models for large organizations. Their successes at our expense were our wake-up call. The American engine of prosperity—huge factories, reductionist use of labor, vertical integration, and mainframe information control—began to stall.

Japan came at America in large part because of its team ethic. In the wake of the war they had no enviable natural resources, no state-of-the-art infrastructure, no money, no computers. What they had was motivated people with a tremendous amount of social capital—the cultural disposition to work together—and the vision and patience to chart a strategy and see it through.

Working largely in teams, the Japanese proceeded to clean our clock. Through the 1970s word wafted across the Pacific Ocean of the new approach the Japanese were using. Instead of asking the least from workers—such as tightening a $\frac{3}{16}$-inch bolt $2\frac{3}{4}$ turns clockwise, over and over and over—the Japanese were asking the most. Every worker, in every function, at every level, was made a part of the company team. And that team's mission was continuous improvement of processes. No idea was too small, and no worker was too small. Everyone participated.

Wm. Edwards Deming, the American statistician who helped get industrial Japan back on its feet in the 1950s, contributed some of the key concepts to the Japanese idea of *kaizen,* or continuous improvement. Foremost among these was the prime directive of teams, the notion that all are human beings. (Years after he returned to the U.S., having received Japan's highest honors, an acquaintance of ours asked him what the Japanese had taught *him.* Deming did not even look up from his dinner to reply. "People are important," he said.)

By the 1990s the new team model overtook the old model of hierarchy, even in the U.S. By the millennium, organizations everywhere, of every size, saw teams as part of the answer to nagging issues of strategic focus, cost containment, restructuring, productivity, training, and connectivity, completing one of the great bloodless revolutions in history, and helping cause the longest period of economic expansion ever.

In the 2000s, the idea of teaming has continued to evolve. Not rapidly, as technology evolves, but incrementally, as people discover new ways to put their heads together, and new reasons to do it. Technology is altering the way teams are expected to work, and occasionally making it easier and more fluid.

The renewed trend toward mergers means that teams will be operating across cultural grains, facing all the accompanying challenges. Already we are seeing virtual organizations that are wholly team-based—ad-hoc organizations thrown together for a single purpose, that do their work, make their money, and then disband.

Likewise, the new generation coming to power, the so-called "N" (for network) Generation, appears to have an intense teaming style all its own, as if they are determined to replace the ego-driven teams of their predecessors. It will be fascinating to see how that plays out.

So teams are here to stay, and even to dominate the way work is performed.

But as we shall see, they are also problematic.

Why Teams?

A team is easily defined: *people doing something together.* It could be a hockey team making a power play, or a research team unraveling an intellectual riddle, or a rescue team pulling a child from a burning building, or a family making a life for itself.

The *something* that a team does isn't what makes it a team; the *together* part is.

Why did the world turn to teams? How could it not? On paper, at least, teams were a no-brainer:

▶ *Teams save money.* In come teams and out goes middle management. Organizations turning to teams solely to save bucks have not been disappointed.

▶ *Teams increase productivity.* Teams are closer to the action and closer to the customer than the old bureaucracy could be. Teams see opportunities for improving efficiencies bosses can't hope to see.

▶ *Teams improve communication.* In a proper team, members are stakeholders in their own success. Teams intensify focus on the task at hand. The very heart of a team, its business if you will, is the sharing of information and the delegation of work.

▶ *Teams do work that ordinary workgroups can't do.* When a task is multifunctional in nature, no single person or crew of functionaries can compete with a team of versatile specialists. There is just too much to know for one person or one discipline to know it all and do it well.

▶ *Teams make better use of resources.* Teams are a way for an organization to focus its most important resource, its brainpower, directly on problems. The team is the Just-In-Time idea applied to organizational structure—the principle that nothing may be wasted.

▶ *Teams mean higher-quality decisions.* Good leadership comes from good knowledge. The essence of the team idea is shared knowledge, and its immediate conversion to shared leadership.

▶ *Teams mean better quality goods and services.* The quality circle (long ago abandoned) was an early expression of the idea that quality improvement requires everyone's best ideas and energies. Teams increase knowledge, and knowledge applied at the right moment is the key to continuous improvement in the quality of goods and services.

▶ *Teams mean improved processes.* Processes occur across functions. Teams, straddling all the functions contributing to a process, have better "process vision." That's why reengineering in the 1990s and the use of teams went hand in hand.

▶ *Teams "differentiate while they integrate."* Most organizations are eager to cut costs and work more effectively, but they worry about the fragmentation that may occur after scaling back. Teams allow organizations to blend people with different kinds of knowledge together; the blend inoculates the organization against the shock of downsizing.

All these things sound really good, and they are all true enough in the aggregate. But teams can also result in a new wave of problems that are causing all kinds of organizations all kinds of grief. For over a decade, we have been discovering that while teams achieve some good outcomes, they often fail for one reason or another.

Yes, companies save dollars by eliminating or combining jobs deemed unnecessary—productivity by attrition. But communication, quality, and true productivity gains—all the promises teams make, and managers get so excited about—remain elusive.

So you can't blame these companies if they are having second thoughts about the team idea. Are teams just another frantic business fashion? Is it time to hitch up the harnesses and rebuild the pyramid of bureaucracy?

No, and no. First, teams are not a fad. They have always been around, and they will always be around. Second, there can be no turning back. The old hierarchy was too expensive. Turning back means taking on the waste and excess costs in industrial bureaucracies that led to the competitiveness calamity in the first place.

We have no choice, except to plunge deeper into the team experience.

But before we do that, it would be wise to stop and ask why teams fail, and how we can change our organizations, or our expectations, so our teams can achieve their promised potential.

The Fork in the Road

Let's finish our history lesson. By the early 1990s, teams were being hailed as the greatest thing since beltless pants. At this point a fork appeared in the road. Companies came to it and, depending on their corporate cultures, veered to the right or to the left.

The two directions have been summed up by global strategist Gary Hamel, who says there are two basic corporate "orientations." These orientations correspond to the numbers above and below the line in any fraction:

$$\frac{2}{3}$$

The top number is the numerator and the bottom number is the denominator. Consider the numerator to be a company's potential for growth, expansion, core competencies, new products, new markets, generativity—profit by doing. The denominator is, by definition, the bottom line—cost containment, downsizing, flattening, delayering, dehiring—profit on paper.

Numerator companies have a vision of creating something terrific and new that didn't exist before. Denominator companies subscribe to a more limited view, a zero-sum picture of mature markets that can never be expanded.

Numerator companies come to the fork in the road and say, "Aha—we can use teams to leverage growth!" Denominator companies come to the same crossing and say, "Aha—we can use the idea of teams to trim the workforce!" (Gary Hamel and C.K. Prahalad, *Competing for the Future,* Cambridge: Harvard Business School Press, 1994.)

This fork in the road explains a lot about team dysfunction. Basically, teams in numerator-type environments experience less dysfunction than teams in denominator-type environments. Teams do well when they are vision-led, and given lots of latitude to let their own genius come to flower. When the creative juices are flowing, you can put up with a lot of baloney. Teams that are a mechanism solely for saving money tend to wear out sooner, their juices flow intermittently at best, and in their frustration, members tear into one another.

The most dysfunctional teams, however, are the in-between teams. They are told they are denominator teams, but in actuality they are numerator teams. Management sells them on the wisdom of teams, pumps up the happy talk, and inspires grand visions of camaraderie and collaboration, and everybody getting along.

In such organizations, teams are a Trojan horse—a fine and wonderful gift wheeled into the gates. But there are Greeks with spears in the belly. So be afraid.

The numerator/denominator split is a false dichotomy in one sense. One is not all good and one all bad. Both numerator and denominator approaches are legitimate. Indeed, most companies pursue both at the same time, tilting back and forth from one to the other. Cost-squeezing initiatives are not innately evil or mean-spirited. They are perfectly defensible in terms of the competition one is up against, in terms of the expectations of shareholders, and in terms of the personalities and experiences of top management—and because wasting is bad.

Nevertheless, when companies whose primary thrust is cost containment come to the fork in the road and choose to use teams primarily as a cost-cutting tactic, they set their teams up for a fall. No team can thrive when it has to forage for its supper. A team is not a money-saving "device." A team isn't any kind of device.

A team is a surprising, perplexing, up-and-down, tragicomic, value-creating human *thing*.

And it is a human thing that needs attention. It has to be pampered, fed, stroked, and have its pen hosed out from time to time. It needs understanding. It needs, at times, something akin to affection. Something old-line bureaucracies, which haven't exactly disappeared, have never been very good at dispensing.

Teams have the potential to do so much more than wring maximum value from a tightly held dollar. When they fail, it is often because the organization employing them has turned to teams in order to trim middle management, without giving the new teams the attention, tools, vision, rewards, or simple clarity that they need to succeed.

This book is about retracing a company's steps to that crucial crossroads, and rethinking the path their teams will take. Numerator, denominator, or (shudder) a hybrid of the two.

Companies approaching teaming with a numerator or growth orientation do not write off the idea of bottom-line profitability. Far from it. There are incredible stories of growth at companies whose top managers have averted their gaze from the mechanical, baseline trance of achieving 9 percent return on investment ("Don't ask how we bring in the 9 percent, just do it!") and focused instead on team processes that are the seedbed for true market expansion.

This is not an item of faith. Look at the stories in the press about which companies are breaking new ground and reaping dividends, and which companies are not. The good companies are noteworthy for their flexibility, focus, speed, and resilience—all team qualities. The second-raters leave a trail of ambiguity wherever they go, because they lack these team qualities. Or worse, they brutalize the teams that could have put them over the top.

A Rosetta Stone

In Egypt during the Napoleonic Wars, a French soldier with a shovel uncovered a clay tablet that explained, in one place, how cuneiform, hieroglyphics, and Greek translated into one another. The find was a windfall for archeologists, who didn't have a clue what all the picture writing of ancient times was trying to say.

We are now going to hand you our Rosetta stone—a book-on-a-stone that explains, in cryptic phrases, everything this book is about. We label this runic wisdom "team intelligence"—everything a team needs to know about itself to survive and succeed.

This chart lists all the reasons teams fail, and the ways in which they can turn failure around.

TEAM INTELLIGENCE

PROBLEM	SYMPTOM	SOLUTION
Mismatched Needs	People with private agendas working at cross-purposes	Get hidden agendas on the table by asking what people want, personally, from teaming
Confused Goals, Cluttered Objectives	People don't know what they're supposed to do, or tasks make no sense	Clarify the reason the team exists; define its purpose and expected outcomes
Unresolved Roles	Team members are uncertain what their job is	Inform team members what is expected of them
Bad Decision Making	Teams may be making the right decisions, but in the wrong way	Choose a decision-making approach appropriate to each decision
Uncertain Boundaries	An empowered team hasn't a clue how empowered it is	Set quantifiable limits to team power
Bad Policies, Stupid Procedures	Team is at the mercy of an employee handbook from hell	Throw away the book and start making sense
Personality Conflicts	Team members do not get along	Learn what team members expect and want from one another; what they prefer; how they differ; start valuing and using differences
Bad Leadership	Leadership is tentative, inconsistent, or stupid	The leader must learn to serve the team and keep its vision alive, or leave leadership to someone else
Bleary Vision	Leadership has foisted a bill of goods on the team	Get a better vision or go away

PROBLEM	SYMPTOM	SOLUTION
Anti-Team Culture	The organization is not really committed to the idea of teams	Team for the right reasons, or don't team at all; never force people onto a team
Insufficient Feedback and Information	Performance is not being measured; team members are groping in the dark	Create a system of free flow of useful information to and from all team members
Ill-Conceived Reward Systems	People are being rewarded for the wrong things	Design rewards that make teams feel safe doing their job; reward teaming as well as individual behaviors
Lack of Team Trust	The team is not a team because members are unable to commit to it	Stop being untrustworthy, or disband or reform the team
Unwillingness to Change	The team knows what to do but will not do it	Find out what the blockage is; use dynamite or Vaseline to clear it

The only problem with our Rosetta stone is that solutions are not as simple as the single-sentence descriptions make them seem. To *utilize* team intelligence, you have to *have* team intelligence. And that is a human learning process involving trial, error, intuition, commitment, honesty, and emotion.

So, sorry—you still have to read the book.

It is useful to remember that all teams—even the most successful—stumble over every one of these problems. Some problems they may never solve.

Nightmare teams, on the other hand, can suffer from every single dilemma and never get one of them right. We have seen teams that have been together three years and longer without making even a dent in improving cohesion.

Chances are your teams occupy the middle ground, doing some things well, but coming up short in a few others. For the moment, use the chart to assess your current teams. You must correctly diagnose your situation, and admit what the problems are, before you can take steps to put them right.

chapter 2

Team Instinct

ou can take the view that the human race is made up entirely of individual loners, each of us making our way by ourselves, all alone in the world.

We don't.

For the most part, we are social creatures. We not only like one another's company, we seek one another out in one situation after another. Deep down, we *need* this interaction, just as we need air, water, and life insurance.

This urge to connect with others is not absolutely universal. There are a few of us, scattered about, who display a lot less need for interaction than the rest of us do. And psychologists and anthropologists have indicated that a dimension of the human psyche does crave solitariness. Some people experience more of this than others.

But most of us thrive on the company of others, and few of us need more than a few hours a week all to ourselves.

The Need for Interaction

We seek from the teams we belong to the same things we seek from other dimensions of life. These are the three As:

1. *Affection.* People living without affection can scarcely be said to be living at all.

2. *Affiliation.* The feeling of belonging to some kind of tribe, organization, or Moose Lodge.

3. *Acknowledgment, and recognition.* Who's to say a tree falling in the wilderness was ever there at all? We need to know we are here, and that others see us.

In teams we also get:

▶ *Exchange of ideas.* The easiest and fastest way to learn is from other people. Without other people, the old wheel must be reinvented again and again and again.

▶ *Personal self-worth.* We see ourselves in terms of other people. Being social is at heart a process of personal benchmarking.

Truth is, despite that particle of us that craves isolation, our sense of ourself withers without contact with others. This is not a platitude; it has been proven many times, throughout history. The process of denying someone access to others—isolation, banishment, banning, scapegoating—has been used for centuries in many cultures as a means of punishment.

Many tribes declared a violator of tribal law a "nonperson." In England, the practice of ignoring someone in disgrace was called "sending them to Coventry"; children were put "in Coventry"—a kind of extended "time out"—for being especially naughty. The Amish still practice a particularly nasty form of isolation called "shunning." Deprived of community, those who are banished quickly die.

Disciplined societies such as police forces, the military, and private schools have long histories of using the mental cruelty of isolation to deal with people who tattle, sabotage, or otherwise undermine the group.

A contemporary example of the need for interaction is the explosion of computer networking. For decades, computer nerds have been isolating themselves in their fascination with technology. Today, suddenly, the isolation has come crashing down; the need for affiliation, for connection, was a driving force behind the development of the Internet.

Remember brainwashing? During the Korean War, it was discovered that you could make POWs believe anything you wanted, simply by cutting them off from interaction with other people. True-blue Eagle Scouts found themselves subscribing, in their lonely torment, to the politics of their jailers.

So, what has this to do with teams? The bright reader has guessed that what was true for the Akkadians in the 21st century B.C. is true for people at AT&T in the 21st century A.D. We still seek to affiliate with others. We still want folks to like us. We still use one another to learn, to achieve complex tasks, and to enhance our individual value as contributors.

Banishment is still the punishment of choice at most organizations. We withhold information ("leave 'em out of the loop"). We isolate their jobs or their physical location ("our man in Murdo Bay"). We attack their credibility so no one is willing to work with them (the pariah syndrome).

Types of Interaction

Affiliation comes in different shades of intensity, and happens for different reasons. Following are various team types—the ways people differ in their ability to join with others and make connections.

▶ *Go-getters.* For these people, the team is the best part of their lives. They adore putting their heads together with others and solving problems. They are in touch with their affiliation needs, and devil take the hindmost.

▶ *Pluggers.* For these people, the team is their ticket to survival— quite literally their paycheck. The team provides the strength of numbers ("They can't fire me—they'd have to fire the whole team.") and, often, foliage to hide their failures or averageness behind. Pluggers put their noses to the stone; and the other people at work, also with their noses to stones, are their team. They will do whatever they must, including team up, to stay alive.

▶ *Doers.* For other people, "stayin' alive" isn't enough. They need more than subsistence, more than a job. They seek a higher level of gratification, a feeling of self-worth, the high of achievement. They want their little lights to shine, and they see their team as the way to do it. Survival-plus.

▶ *Homebodies.* Work versus home is an issue. People getting their affiliation needs met at home—the marriage-as-team and the family-as-team—will often fall into the plugger camp at work. People not getting their affiliation needs met at home will see the workplace as the place to find this satisfaction. There are people so fulfilled by their role as team members that they wind up on scores of different teams, at work and in the community.

▶ *Loners.* Then there are people not getting their affiliation needs met at either end, home or work. Often they are dying inside, unable to team effectively, despite hungering to do so. They are the barstool-sitters of life, unable to come in off the sidelines and join in. If you have one on your team, keep the ball away from him.

▶ *Killers.* Others, toxic loners, have no wish at all to team, and actively seek to destroy the team. They would prefer seeing their colleagues killed by stinging insects to linking heart and soul to them.

One reason teams fail is that the people on the team have widely differing social needs. A go-getter paired off with a killer is a recipe not for teamwork, but for beef Wellington.

The point of this is not to demonize or marginalize the loners and killers. Most everyone has some teaming capacity, and can be led to do his or her best. But most of us *need* to affiliate, and we equate it with survival. That is a powerful force, and team leaders who don't make note of it, and use it in their team building, miss out on a big opportunity.

Remember that what you are attempting is not something artificial, or a management fad. We have always teamed. It was the heart of the hunt, hundreds of thousands of years ago. It was the heart of early agriculture, 50,000 years ago. Teaming is in our blood. We want to do it and do it well. But we have this tendency, because of our other human compulsions, to muck it up in the execution.

When the going gets rough on your team, never lose sight of this inner longing. Remember that nearly everyone's intentions are good at heart, and that working together as a group is very, very natural.

chapter 3

Individual Needs vs. Team Needs

B esides differing in degrees of teaming instinct, people on teams differ in terms of personal agendas.

We make a big deal out of team objectives. Team objectives are supposed to be powerful visions that unite the members of a team and drive them on irresistibly to success.

But guess what—in teaming physics, the team objective is decidedly the weak force. The strong force remains the collection of personal wishes and wants that team members bring to the team.

Just because we are attracted to teaming up doesn't mean we set our other desires on the shelf. We don't know about you, but we'll be doggoned if we'll forsake our personal dreams for the sake of some workgroup.

So a conflict exists between individual team members' goals and the overarching goal of the team itself.

And it can play out very painfully. Imagine a team of four, with the acknowledged goal of creating an e-commerce site for a conventional business—let's say consumer gardening supplies. The goal is simple: reengineer a local business to cyberspace.

The four team members are Doug, a freelance programmer; Edie, an in-house graphic designer; Miller, an outsider brought in to help develop a catalog; and Avram, an old-guard sales engineer with major ESOP holdings in the business this project will some day supplant.

Sounds workable. But the four people aren't stick figures. They each have an agenda that is subtly pulling the team apart.

Doug is upset because he has a program from a previous job that he feels would be fine for this job, with a few minor alterations. His agenda is to finish his part of the project and get on to the next one. Frankly, he needs the money. But his teammates won't give him the go-ahead to do this.

Edie is usually a good sport on teams, redoing work at their request. But Edie has a secret. She's going to have a baby in seven months. It's too early to tell everyone—she doesn't want to count her chicken until it's hatched. But her mind is on that baby, and the project just doesn't do much for her. Her best design so far has been a garden page featuring characters from Peter Rabbit.

Miller thinks he's God's gift to catalog consulting. His taste in teamwork is to come in every day with a new plan, a major overhaul, a fresh vision. He's driving everyone crazy. People don't know this, but Miller is a recovering alcoholic going through a manic period. He's having the time of his life, getting interested in his career just as others are easing out of theirs.

Avram is the Mustache Pete of the team. He helped start the company years ago, and he has reservations about the whole Internet thing. He read something in the paper, a year ago, that no one is making money there. It was his last fresh insight. Secretly, he resents the bright but uncommitted youngsters around him, and lapses into frequent lectures on the virtue of selling garden supplies off the back of a pickup truck. He feels unappreciated, and his lectures are a misguided effort to show people what is inside him.

We've just described four decent, talented people who are not in any way opposed to working on teams, and have nothing major against one another. But there are numerous conflicts between their individual goals and the team goal, and these conflicts will only build in significance.

They probably won't ever blow up, or go ballistic, or melt down into headline dysfunctionality. But they'll never gel as a team, and they won't meet their goals in a timely fashion, and the website will be a joke, because their team goals were deep-sixed by a raft of unfulfilled personal goals.

Doug, Edie, Miller, and Avram are just not going to click. Not for lack of good intentions. But their good intentions, taken together, are a feeble force compared to their individual, unaddressed needs.

Rebalancing the Load

Effective teamwork means a continual balancing act between meeting team needs and individual needs. We're not just talking here about the basic human need for survival through affiliation with others that we discussed in the last chapter. We are speaking of all the things that each of us wants, things that have nothing to do with teams or jobs.

While it's nice to be around other folks and work with them, we are, all of us, still looking out for Number One. Forget all the movie scenes of the scrappy doughboy jumping on a live grenade to save his buddies in uniform. In real life, we take actions with others primarily to satisfy our own personal agendas. People will only agree to team if it meets their own needs first.

Of course, there are some of us who live for deferred gratification as a masochistic kick, who may agree to work toward a team outcome now in exchange for some personal outcomes later on. These people happily forestall today's druthers in order to incur payback tomorrow.

But, in general, it's a "me first," or at least a "please consider my needs while we meet the team's," kind of world.

Find the Agenda

"Good soldiers" are sometimes not soldiers at all. Teams must be leery of members who have no honest intention to be working members of the team. In their hearts, they may be saying:

"I'm not here to work with the team, but to take credit for its successes."

"I'm not here to work with the team, but to associate with some of its members."

"I'm not here to work with the team, but to use it as a steppingstone to better things."

The term "hidden agenda" was coined to describe this kind of covert careerism. It is not honest and it is very destructive to team coherence. Good team members recognize that in order to build trust, they must uncover their own hidden agendas and expose them to the light of day.

In our hypothetical team, everyone has to put their agendas on the table for the others to examine.

Edie, Miller, and Avram need to be apprised of Doug's frustration. Chances are they will empathize with his need to finish up and move on, and move more quickly. Perhaps, with their empathy under his belt, Doug will relax a bit and let the project find its own rhythm.

Even if Edie does not tell Doug, Miller, and Avram about her pregnancy, she needs to communicate to them that something is cooking that is pulling her from the work. It's possible that she isn't the best person for the team, and she may have to be replaced. Hey, it happens.

Miller needs to be told that he's making people crazy. It doesn't have to be cruel. Telling Miller why others are ambivalent about the project should engage him, and modulate his excesses. It wouldn't hurt for them to learn why he's so excited, either—it's much bigger than a love of catalog sales.

And Avram—poor Avram—needs to open up and respect his teammates more. He's so connected to the company of ten years ago that it prevents him from being here now in a useful way. He should tell his story, and then he should shut up. One lesson of teaming is that one is never too old to grow up.

Only by processing through each team member's wishes and wants, and at the very minimum acknowledging their validity, can the group redirect its focus—which has suddenly grown more intense and deep with knowledge—at the team goal.

And make the best damn gardening supplies website the world ever saw.

Who is to say that the team mission is the only mission a team can acknowledge and pursue? Deep down, most of us are not especially good soldiers, and we do not long to subordinate our own desires to the common good. Live grenades do not get leaped on routinely.

On the contrary: sacrifice, loyalty, and the willingness to go through a little hell for one another occur only when cards are on the table, and people are allowed (and required) to be honest about their needs.

Personal goals that prevent us from achieving team goals are often very honorable:

▶ having a baby

▶ spending more time with family

▶ seeking a better job after this one

▶ going back to school and getting that degree

Or they can be a shade less edifying:

▶ making a name for oneself

▶ joining a team that is clearly funded

▶ wanting to belong to a team of "winners" for a change

▶ wanting a group that one can dominate

▶ glomming onto a team that has already achieved successes

▶ hiding behind a powerful executive's support and championship

Whatever the personal goals, we need to know what they are and to deal with them or at least acknowledge them as a team—perhaps even to make them corollary team goals. When we know our fellow team members want us to achieve what we ourselves want, that is a terrific bond between members.

The sooner we know one another's personal needs and hopes, the better for the team. This doesn't mean that personal needs have to be completely met first before true teaming can get underway. It does mean that acknowledging and addressing these needs as a group, early on, can help prevent our "selfish" desires from sinking the team effort.

chapter 4

Teamwork vs. Socialwork

Here's yet another level in which goals and needs get confused. It's a category of goals we call "socialwork." Socialwork is a perversion of the need to affiliate. In it, affiliation breaks free from the team objective—it is just affiliating for the fun of affiliating.

In the Stone Age, socialwork was when one caveman kept interrupting stalking the woolly mammoth to do the woolly mammoth dance. This drove the other cavemen nuts, because everyone knows you kill the mammoth first, then do your impression of it later, around the fire.

A hundred thousand years later, teams are still afflicted, at every turn, with outbreaks of the mammoth dance.

All too often, the problem isn't just one "class clown" who can't stick to the task—it's a major contingent of fun-lovers who kill the work ethic dead. Two people with lampshades on their heads can kill any serious enterprise.

The stated purpose for a team is to gather people together and collaborate on jointly accomplishing agreed-upon team outcomes; i.e., get things done together. The purpose of socialwork, on the other hand, is to get your personal needs for affiliation met by being involved in a group.

One is work-related, and results in a dead mammoth. The other is a goof, and likely results in no mammoth, or worse, a very undead one.

Here are examples of teamwork attractions that distract members from the true team goal:

▶ the team has some super-attractive members

▶ the team has a charismatic leader

▶ the team gets to travel

▶ the team has an incredible expense account

▶ the team was written up in *Fortune*

▶ the team gets a great workspace

▶ the team does no lifting

▶ the team goes to Vail every February

This is a mixed list, but what it says is that there are more reasons for joining a team than just the human need to interact or the validity of the stated team goal ("develop a manned flight rocket to travel to the Sun"). Knowing these things about one another, up front, can resolve anxieties and expectations before they drag the team down.

Sometimes the line between teamwork and socialwork gets a bit fuzzy. You can usually tell this is happening when everyone on a team is pissed off. An example of the teamwork/socialwork clash is when Team Member A is working on a task while Team Members B, C, and D are in the next cubicle chatting away about non-work-related things. While A is doing teamwork, B, C, and D are doing socialwork.

It is a uniquely human conflict—work vs. play. While play is natural and normal, it quickly becomes corrosive when play replaces work as the goal for one or more team members. It will not take long for Team Member A to resent the fun the others are having, and their unwillingness to pull their share of the load.

Conversely, Members B, C, and D will feel genuinely indignant and angry that their socializing is not perceived as the vital glue that holds the team together. Hint: If glue isn't being attached to every team member, it isn't vital glue.

A survey a few years back suggested that during an average workday, at least one-fourth of the time is occupied by socialwork. The researchers also suggested that this mental break time is a necessary component to staying sane at work (relieving stress). The problems occur when some people on a team are teaming at the same time others on the same team are socializing.

While both teamwork and socialwork are essential to team success, getting the whole team in sync is important.

Plus, some team members have higher needs in one end of the spectrum than the other. Some people never seem to need or want a break, while others don't appear to be pulling their weight since they're usually schmoozing.

All work and no play makes you dull. All play and no work makes you unemployed.

part two

Where Teams Go Wrong

▼

c h a p t e r 5

Misplaced Goals, Confused Objectives

he last three chapters were about valid team objectives having to duke it out with the objectives of individual team members. This chapter is about team objectives that are suspect all by themselves.

How many times have you heard colleagues say this: "The boss has given us such unrealistic objectives."

They are really saying one of three things:

1. *They don't believe in the outcome.* The boss is famous for his five-year plan. But no one has paid any real attention to it in, oh, five years.

2. *They don't believe the outcome is reachable.* Maybe the boss is blowing blue smoke again, pulling figures out of a hat. Worse, maybe she read an article about "stretch goals," and has the bright idea of stretching us to meet the goals.

3. *They can't figure out what the boss really wants as an outcome.* Teams fail when their reason for being is unclear. The goal is expressed complicatedly, ambiguously—in dollars, in eliminated defects, in market share, in new customers. How do you focus simultaneously on four focal points?

If your team doesn't know where it's going or what it wants the outcome to be, your best remaining option is to have everyone fall to their knees and beg the stampede to step lightly over you.

Barring divine intervention, however, your next best option is to achieve clarity on the outcome you're after, such as:

"Our desired outcome is to create a leakproof disposable diaper before the snow flies."

"Our desired outcome is to have fewer customers make remarks about our mothers."

"Our desired outcome is to be so good at everything we do that we drive our competitor to existential despair."

Leaders, Visions, Goals

The three objectives above are admittedly flip. But they have the virtue of describing not just what the outcome is, but how you will know when you have achieved it, and what it will feel like. They have a human sound, which is good, because teams are made up of human beings.

To understand the length, breadth, depth, and pH of the pickle a team without clear objectives is in, you must understand the inner nature of a goal or objective. The soul of the goal, if you will. Like a cinder kept alive to kindle new fire, the soul of the goal is kindled and communicated by the leader.

A goal is not a number. Wm. Edwards Deming, who knew more about human motivation than a boatload of organizational behaviorists, was very clear, in his famous Fourteen Points, that numerical targets and quotas do more damage than they do good.

A proper goal hones in on what we have been discussing—the natural disposition of people to work together on teams. It begins with the vision of the leader that a task is desirable and performable, in human terms. The leader may be a member of the team or a core of members within the team, or may even function primarily outside the team. But he or she (or they) must have credibility within the team.

The vision is translated by credible leadership into a concrete aspiration. Concrete means real, visionable, something that, when you hear it, you can almost taste.

John F. Kennedy said, *"We will put a man on the moon."* That sentence explains almost everything you need to know about leadership and goals. It is clear. It is significant. And it engages.

A leader whose goals are constantly shifting is no leader at all. A stated goal stabilizes and concentrates the vision of the leader into something that is clear and concise, and that represents a continuing vision of what the team hopes to achieve together. A good vision is an act of faith that a difficult, worthwhile goal can be achieved.

If the goal is clear enough and engages people's hearts as well as their minds, the goal itself assumes much of the burden of leadership. It's so good it lives on its own. It becomes a continuing corrective against distraction, confusion, and decay.

Most goals aren't that good, though. *"We will put a man in a station wagon"* is clear and performable, but lacks oomph.

If you work in a big company, in the middle somewhere, a team goal is not the same as a strategic goal. Strategic goals properly call for ambitious, broad, long-range achievement. Team goals tend to have a more modest ring to them. (If they don't, conduct the chew-check: check to see that the team isn't biting off more than it can chew. If it isn't performable, it's not a good goal.)

A good team goal has several parts:

▶ a *task*—what are you doing;

▶ a promised *limit* of what you're doing—unlike the enchanted brooms in *The Sorcerer's Apprentice,* you know when to stop;

▶ a promised *level of performance*—you'll spare no expense; you'll stick to a tight budget; it will be world-class work; "good enough" is good enough;

▶ a *deadline*—a sunset clause, after which even the best coach reverts to the role of pumpkin; and

▶ the definition of the *customer*—who all this effort is for.

As a final thought, remember that actions toward outcomes don't happen in a vacuum. Large organizations with lots of teams have lots of objectives bobbling about. The death knell for teams in such companies is when the objectives of all the teams never fit together into a grand *uber*-objective.

It's like the cartoon of the two railroad companies meeting in Utah to drive the golden spike, and discovering they have laid different gauges of track. If team objectives don't fit together, somebody screwed up big-time.

Goal Wars

Harvey recalls an experience from a few years back, at one of the larger and more prestigious bomb factories in our nation, back when we knew who the enemy was. Trouble was brewing because of a lack of linked goals. The company had just won a contract for an advanced weapons system. This weapon was so complicated, so sophisticated, so cutting-edge, that making it required seven separate teams—each team working on a different part of this multi-tank-killing minirocket, code-named Fluffy.

In theory, Fluffy had enough punch to cause a twelve-story building to disintegrate. The potential of the system out on the battlefield was mindblowing. Equally mindblowing, however, were the conniption fits the seven teams experienced trying to design and assemble a prototype.

The problems began at the goal stage. Thrilled with the technological opportunity at hand, the seven teams huddled separately and worked on their end of the problem. Management endorsed this idea, likening it to the skunkworks model used to great success elsewhere. Like a scavenger hunt, each team was instructed to pool its best ideas and meet at the end of a two-month period in an idea-sharing progress meeting. As the date drew near there was a sense of excitement in the air. That morning the room was atingle with engineerial delight.

Each team got to report on its part of the project to date. The first team got up to speak and with great pride explained their innovative approach to opening the flaps covering the launch tube. As they spoke, there was a rumble from some of the other teams. One person stood up and yelled at the speaker, "You idiot, if you do that, your flaps will cover up our sights and we can't see what we're shooting at." Another team chair chimed in, "Our electronics array hasn't been designed to do that!" Etc., etc., etc.

Remarkably, the meeting went downhill from there. Recriminations, reprisals, faces slapped, duels arranged at dawn in the marshy area down by the bullet casings shed. Months of product development time and many millions of dollars were lost because of unlinked goals. It took an additional two months for respective team members to overcome their anger and multidirectional finger pointing.

Lack of goal integration caused their project to . . . disintegrate.

Goal Sadism

Another team excess to guard against is goal sadism. There are various degrees of rigor you can expose your team to. On one end of the spectrum you can make life too cozy for your team. Peel their grapes, talcum their bottoms, etc. But pampering's no good—teams thrive on a certain degree of anxiety.

The opposite extreme of pummeling teams to perform, however, can be horrific. We have known managers and team leaders who were psychopathic in their willingness to cause team pain.

Take the phrase "stretch goal." It is a perfectly legitimate idea, simply an ambitious goal you set for organizational performance. Motorola's goal of Six Sigma errorlessness (limiting quality defects to 2 or 3 per million outputs) was a stretch goal. Difficult, but as Motorola has proven, achievable in some areas without massive bloodshed.

But there are individuals out there who focus not on what is achievable but on how much it stretches the team. In their minds a stretch goal would be a fivefold increase in team productivity. It was painless for them to utter the goal at a team meeting, but oh, the pain it caused team members in the year that followed.

We knew a manager in Minnesota who joked about his motivational methodology. "I chase 'em up a ladder, then I kick it out from under 'em." Nice guy.

Larry Bossidy of Allied Signal created a famous metaphor of the "burning platform." Until people are informed there is a crisis (like, your oil platform is on fire) you cannot get them to do the difficult thing (jump overboard and swim to safety). It is a great metaphor for understanding motivation. But some managers take it to the next stage, and are setting their platforms on fire in order to chase teams over the edge.

It should be every organization's goal, in as long a term as possible, to survive. But manufacturing short-term crises that kill today's teams in order to achieve a long-term goal—well, it isn't very nice.

The Road to Nowhere

Teams seeking to create trust and instill a sense of strong leadership must clearly define and then link their objectives. This isn't a maybe, it's a you *have* to. After all, if you don't know where you're going, any road will take you there.

No two roads are alike, of course. When a team is assigned a task, it feels lucky to be placed in an orderly environment. It's more pleasant cruising down a four-lane highway than warily hacking a footpath through the jungle. But many assignments put teams squarely in the jungle—creating something from nothing; creating (and this is often worse) something from something; building bridges between different ideas, cultures, products, teams; cleaning up the messes previous teams made.

Work is often confusing, cluttered, and inconvenient. And people are always people, with all the variation and inconsistency that humanity implies.

Given the inherent disorder of most team tasks, teams must insist on diamond-like clarity at the onset of a mission, with a hard-edged understanding of the impending task.

Goal-setting by the Spoonful

Goal-setting often fails because people get hung up on the long-term aspect of the primary goal. "Retake Granada," was an overarching goal that took Spain 500 years. It might have been achieved quicker had *El Objecto Mejor* been broken down into component minigoals from the start.

That is what proper goal-setting is—you start with a grand supergoal, that the entire team is striving for, and then you chart a path toward achieving it, with team members assigned to a series of linked, doable, short-term steps.

Successful teams live and breathe in the short term. That is where the action is, and that is where intelligence is put to work. They may plan longer term, but they act for the present.

They also concentrate on a few goals at a time. New teams are famous for declaring 30 goals or outcomes when they first come together. Some organizations require the creation of a list of every action a person is to perform during the next performance cycle— maybe a year, maybe longer. This is what passes for long-term vision in many organizations.

The problem is that when confronted with a list of 20 to 30 objectives, the tendency of most sentient beings is to go into shock and do nothing for a period of recovery. The human brain is a dazzling organ, but not even people with brains in good working order can work on more than two objectives at the same time.

Goals that are not being worked on at present tend to gnaw at one's mental innards. This decreases productivity. We may state this as a rule: the more goals and objectives a team is handed, the worse its performance will be.

Despite master plans to the contrary, things have a way of changing. Allow for flexibility as time passes, for the list of goals and objectives to be amended as new knowledge leads to new understanding. One of the horrors of organizations is seeing an individual confronted by a manager for the noncompletion of goals that anyone who has been paying attention knows are no longer relevant.

Goal Sludge

The short term is where it's at. Not "Retake Granada," but "Start with that blue row-house on Seville Street, the one with white shutters." Focusing on the doable allows a team to achieve instant, perfect understanding, and to strike quickly, like commandos.

So what constitutes short?

We begin by proposing task durations much shorter than you may currently use as benchmarks. We sort all goals and objectives into short-, mid-, and long-term timeframes. Short means less than one month (like next week); mid means one to three months; long means three to six months.

So much for the vaunted 100-year plan. But that is just the point—anything beyond six months takes you into the realm of pipe dreaming and strategic planning. Too many things can go wrong, or change. One little bend in the river can wipe out months of work, and devastate morale.

If you have a goal pushing beyond the six-month limit, break it down into shorter-term tasks that fit into these three timeframes. That way the team is continuously knocking down fresh goals and objectives, experiencing successes, staying on track, moving quickly, and raising team motivation.

Commando teams are small, single goal, and short term. When their goal is accomplished, they disband back into the larger organization, only to be regrouped again into other short-term action teams.

Once a team lists its goals and objectives and sorts them into the appropriate timeframes, the team must then prioritize the short list. If a task doesn't appear on the high-priority, short-term goals/objectives list, the hell with it. *Leave all the rest behind.*

As time passes and midterm goals/objectives move into the short period, reprioritize the new short list. If the goals/objectives at the bottom of the priority list are still there when the team reprioritizes, then repeat what you did before—ignore them. Under no circumstances are you to complete these tasks. You are hereby forbidden even to worry about them—which you might well do without our strict instructions.

There is an obscure phrase in psychology for the tension caused by unresolved, uncompleted tasks—the Zygarnic Effect, after Bluma Zygarnic, the Brooklyn psychologist who first described the phenomenon. Uncompleted tasks slowly paralyze individuals and teams—until the simple act of getting together to discuss progress looms insurmountably.

The result of uncompleted tasks is: *goal sludge.* Goal sludge is not bad or evil, but it engenders anxiety and lassitude. It must be dealt with, and quickly. An unfulfilled goal can be given a higher, more emphatic priority. It can be allotted a longer time horizon for completion, or a shorter one, if that helps. It can be "shared" with people who have more expertise or energy or freshness for the task. It can be delegated to someone else—fresh horses! It can be outsourced completely—"Handle it!"

But the sludge must be disposed of somehow. Or else it lies there, in everyone's sight and nostrils, stinking in the desert sun, with tomato plants sprouting out of it.

Extricate yourself from its sludgy power, however, and the difference is day and night. It's like freeing up a gigabyte of disk space, or like taking a two-week vacation at home. Thank God almighty, you're free at last.

The Final Element

One final element is critical to good goal-setting—passion.

The world is full of boring visions. Whole organizations drag themselves from quarterly report to quarterly report pursuing them. It is as if the leadership has read all the right books, and made up its mind not to make any obvious mistakes, but neglected to make the goal interesting in any way.

A dull goal lacks originality, personality, sizzle. A good goal goes beyond setting a numerical target or quota, and beyond some lame mission-statement language about becoming world-class, or best-in-breed, or worm-free, or whatever the fad phrase in the planning community is this week.

People want to be turned on by their work. A good goal gives them something to respond to. Something to buy into and claim ownership over. When a goal is really good, it doesn't just belong to you. A transformation occurs, and you belong to it. It makes you proud and humble, both at the same time.

chapter 6

Bad Decision Making

There was a time in his life, back around 1970, when Mike worked as an autoclave technician at a large metropolitan hospital. Though he worked the graveyard shift, he was still astonished at the military orderliness of the sterile laboratory's work regimen. The shift supervisor watched everything like a hawk, and clocked every tray that went in or out. She and she alone filled out all requisition forms. She kept these forms on a clipboard, which she passed on at sunrise to the day shift manager replacing her. Not only was Mike not allowed to make decisions, *she* wasn't allowed to. It was strict.

One night, when the supervisor was on break, a nurse came dashing down the hall, in urgent need of a scrub set for some procedure. Mike swallowed hard and handed it to her, without filling out the usual paperwork. The next day he was fired for allowing supplies to leave the area without paperwork. He had to turn in his Foley clamps and surgical mask. It was all very sad. But Mike was philosophical—at least some motorcycle accident victim up in the ER got the asphalt cleaned out of his wound.

This was a case of too-tight central control causing the team to fail in its stated mission of helping patients. The way a team *decides to decide* is one of the most important decisions it makes. You may want to read this last sentence again. It is not a misprint.

Teams start by learning, and they hit their stride when they act. How action is triggered varies according to the action in question. Right decisions are decided the right way. And vice versa: Napoleon's choice to duke it out with Wellington at Waterloo was not just a bad decision, it was the battle; it was the whole war.

What's even more dangerous in the long term is consistently relying on the wrong process to arrive at decisions. How did Napoleon decide to head into the trap awaiting him on the Flemish plains? He just decided, all by himself, that's how. It was the Napoleonic way.

Perhaps, if he had shown a bit of executive flexibility and followed another method of decision making, he and his team in arms might have had a better day on the field. He had seven options, each one suitable for a specific kind of situation. Napoleon, being an autocrat, would only have been amenable to a couple of the decision-making approaches. Your team, over the weeks and months of working together, may have to use them all.

▶ **Consensus.** Consensus decision making is where all team members get a chance to air their opinions and must ultimately agree on the outcomes. If any team member does not agree, discussions continue. Compromise must be used so that every team member can agree with and commit to the outcome.

Advantages: Produces an innovative, creative, high-quality decision; elicits commitment by all members to implement the decision; uses the resources of all members; the future decision-making ability of the team is enhanced.

Disadvantages: Takes a lot of time and psychological energy, and a high level of member skill. Time pressure must be minimal. There can be no emergency in progress. Bring pajamas—you could be doing this all night.

▶ **Majority Rule.** Majority decision making is democracy in action. The team votes, the majority wins. Simple.

Advantages: Can be used when there's no time for a full-dress consensus decision, or when the decision is not so important that consensus is necessary, and when 100-percent member commitment is critical for implementing the decision; closes discussion on issues that are not highly important for the team.

Disadvantages: Usually leaves an alienated minority, a time bomb for future team effectiveness; important talents of minority team members may be snubbed; commitment for implementing the decision is only partially present; full benefit of team interaction does not happen.

▶ **Minority Rule.** Minority decision making usually takes the form of a subcommittee of a larger team that investigates information and makes recommendations for action.

Advantages: Can be used when not everyone can get together to make a decision; when the team is in a time crunch and must delegate responsibility to a committee; when only a few members have relevant expertise or knowledge; when broader team commitment is not needed to implement the decision; useful for simple, routine decisions.

Disadvantages: Does not utilize the talents of all team members; does not build broad commitment for implementing the decision; unresolved conflict and controversy may damage future team effectiveness; not much benefit from team interaction.

▶ **Averaging.** Averaging is the epitome of compromise; it is how our esteemed Congress decides: team members haggle, bargain, cajole, and negotiate an intentional middle position. Usually no one is happy with the result except the moderates on the team.

Advantage: Individual errors and extreme opinions tend to cancel each other out, making this a better method than "authority rule without discussion."

Disadvantages: Opinions of the least knowledgeable members may annul the opinions of the most knowledgeable members. Little team involvement in the decision making, so commitment to the decision will likely be weak. Letting members with the greatest expertise make the decision is almost always better than a group average.

▶ **Expert.** This is simple. Find or hire experts, listen to what they say, and follow their recommendations.

Advantages: Useful when the expertise of one person is so far superior to that of all other team members that little is gained by discussion; should be used when the need for membership action in implementing the decision is slight.

Disadvantages: How do you determine who the best expert is? No commitment is built for implementing the decision; advantages of team interaction are lost; resentment and disagreement may result in sabotage and deterioration of team effectiveness; knowledge and skills of other team members are not used.

▶ **Authority Rule Without Discussion.** This is where there is usually no room for discussion; where predetermined decisions are handed down from higher authority. Moses on Mt. Sinai. Trust is often killed with this method, as when a team leader tries to fool team members into thinking that their opinions about the decision really affect the decision. Team members know when a team leader is jerking them around.

Advantages: Applies more to administrative needs, useful for simple, routine decisions; should be used when very little time is available to make the decision; when team members expect the designated leader to make the decision; and when team members lack the skills or information to make the decision anyway.

Disadvantages: One person cannot be a good resource for every decision; advantages of team interaction are lost; zero team commitment is developed for implementing the decision; resentment and disagreement may result in sabotage and deterioration of team effectiveness; resources of other team members are not used.

▶ **Authority Rule With Discussion.** This method is also known as Participative Decision Making. Unfortunately, most people don't know what this really means. Many leaders think it means they have to give up their decision-making responsibility. Not true. Under this method, those in the decision-making role make it clear from the onset that the task of decision making is theirs. Then they join in a lively discussion of the issues; their opinions count just like those of other team members. When they have heard enough to make an educated decision, they cut off the discussion, make the decision, then get back to all team members to let them know how their inputs affected their decision. Most team members feel listened to and willing to participate in another team decision using this method.

Advantages: Gains commitment from all team members. Develops a lively discussion on the issues using the skills and knowledge of all team members. Is clear on who is ultimately accountable for the decision of the team.

Disadvantages: Requires good communication skills on the part of team members; requires a leader willing to make decisions.

Though fashion occasionally underscores one or another of these approaches, there is no right or wrong way to decide an issue. The important thing is that *the team must decide, in advance, what decision-making method will be used.* No surprises. If members are apprised of the process, even autocratic methods acquire the consent and blessing of all.

chapter 7

Empowerment Uncertainties

Between the subjects of the last two chapters, goal setting and decision making, is an enormous crevasse, into which teams fall, then fester and stink up the joint. This is the area of boundary management—or in the case of team failure, mismanagement.

Empowerment is a form of decision making not mentioned in the last chapter because it involves individual, not team decisions. Yet it is probably the most important kind of deciding that occurs on teams.

Here's the deal: Organizations create teams to achieve certain goals. They may tell the teams, usually quite vaguely, that they are "empowered" to some degree to do whatever is necessary to achieve the goal.

Or they may not.

Either way, the team has been set up to fail. Either the team feels it has no authority or leverage to carry out its mission, or it is confused about what its authority or leverage really amounts to.

It is deeply depressing to a team to go to all the trouble of learning how to solve a problem, only to be paralyzed, unable to implement that solution, because it doesn't know if it's allowed to. Or worse, to implement the wrong (but defensible) solution because it doesn't think management will go for the right (but ambitious) one.

On the other hand, it is terrifying for management to empower people to make decisions in advance without any assurance those decisions will be sensible or defensible. Many an empowered team, thinking its decision-making authority to be vast and absolute, learns to its chagrin that its empowerment was really more of an expression, a figure of speech, than a blank check.

Some managers "empower" teams to "be nice"; then when the team actually goes and does something on its own, something different than the managers would have done, they learn the high price of nice.

It is a drag on both sides when managers believe they have instructed a team to make decisions, only to find out later that the team didn't believe a word of it. The team gets into trouble, which was what it was trying to avoid, and now the manager has less reason to trust the team than before.

Obviously, teams and managers need some sort of arbitration, so that there are things teams can do to advance their cause without jeopardizing the larger organization's security.

So, what can be done?

First, write the word *empowerment* on a clean sheet of paper, fold the sheet carefully into sixteenths, and then chuck it in the wastebasket.

From now on, instead of empowerment, think in terms of the phrase *boundary management*. For there can be no empowering without defining what the power is, who has it, where it starts, and where it ends.

Boundary management is a method for negotiating and agreeing to a set of constraints or boundaries within which team members are free to make decisions on their own. These boundaries will vary depending on the degree of experience or expertise of each team member.

They also vary depending on the relationship the team leader or manager has with each team member. If you are confident about a team member's judgment or competence, you will give him or her more latitude than someone who just walked in off the street.

The empowerment grid states explicitly and concretely what each team member has authority to do. If an act is not specified in the grid, the team member must consult with others before acting.

The Empowerment Grid

	RESOURCES $5,000 budget cash costs, people costs	
QUANTITY For group of 120 customers	**OBJECTIVE** Create a training workshop	**SCHEDULE** June 1–21
	QUALITY Professional quality—this is for outside consumption!	

The most common parameters or constraints around which boundaries are created are resources, schedule, quantity, and quality.

The team leader fills in the center square—the *objective* the team must accomplish. In our example, the team task is to create a training workshop. The objective in the center of the grid is usually non-negotiable: you gotta do it. Question is, and the other boxes provide the answers, how you gonna do it?

Now the leader creates a *target* for each of the constraints, as a starting point for the negotiation. Under resources, you may put down a cash budget of $5,000, plus a week's time from two team members.

For *schedule,* you may enter a start date of June 1 and a completion date of June 21.

The *quantity* dimension is straightforward enough—how big a project is it?

The *quality* constraint may take a bit longer to negotiate since it's, well, qualitative. Here you try to describe what the outcome should look like in as much detail as possible. Everyone must put into words his or her as-yet-unarticulated vision of what the project will be like.

For example, what outcome do you expect for the workshop—more efficient work processes? Also, you should describe in some detail what the workshop will look and feel like. Will it be a professional-quality slideshow, enhanced by outside subcontractors? A simpler in-house PowerPoint job? Or will typewritten handouts be good enough?

Be specific here. Give both positive and negative examples to help the team members understand what is acceptable and what is not. For example, specify that if handouts are OK, they can't be smudged-over tenth-generation photocopies—at a bare minimum they must be legible. If you take the slide presentation route, specify if custom photos will be required, or if clip art is good enough.

Before moving forward, the grid must be negotiated with the team. Maybe the leader has miscalculated, or the team can assert that another way is better, or cheaper, or quicker, or more appropriate.

For each constraint, the team members and team leader negotiate the range within which the team member may make independent decisions without having to go back and check with the leader.

The leader knows what's acceptable as an outcome—the big picture. The team members will have opinions based on their closer-to-the-ground perspective.

For the resource constraint, for example, the leader may recommend that at least $3,000 should be used—because the team must spend that much to ensure refunding at the same level next year. For the same reason, one team member may want to push spending levels to $10,000—use it or lose it, right? And such a well-funded slideshow would be a guaranteed success.

But the leader may say no, because spending $10,000 for a presentation on corporate responsibility would rain hellfire upon them all.

The beauty of the empowerment grid is that as things change, and they will, you are forced to go back and check the validity of all of the constraints. It's like a project compass, to keep you from veering the wrong way due to some fuzzy notion of empowerment, and sailing off the edge of the map.

The point is that before proceeding with a project, team members must know precisely what lengths they may go to without having to ask for permission. This saves time, reduces frustration, restores confidence and calm, and eliminates the thing we most dread on teams—surprises.

c h a p t e r   8

Unresolved Roles

hen we were kids, we didn't worry about roles and responsibilities. We swarmed through the neighborhood, doing what we pleased or what we were told, until we got distracted and did something else. We were an army without ranks, a tribe of generalists, a corporation without job titles—a nonhierarchical, de-layered, super-flattened, inverted-pyramid, matrix/cluster mob. And we liked it.

Fast-forward to the preteam era, the 1960s and 1970s, and the workplace was lousy with roles. Every worker had a job description. Every job description described exactly what a worker's tasks, roles, and working relationships were. Both, as a rule, were defined quite narrowly—second-level lab technician, plastics; assistant to first-level lab technician, plastics.

But in the team era of the '90s, job descriptions became less precise, broader. Roles are now hardly mentioned on paper. But these roles and relationships, whether committed to print or not, play important roles in successful teaming.

Implicit in the idea of teams is that *people are adults.* We're too grown up for the pigeonholing of conventional job descriptions and scientific management. However, many teams, in their new freedom, have reverted to swarming through the neighborhood.

They are doing what they want to do, or what they are good at. Important but less desirable work is not getting done.

Somehow, team members must have three conditions in effect:

1. All members must know the task they must complete . . .

2. Without those roles and responsibilities becoming straightjackets, and cutting off circulation to the brain . . .

3. While making sure that all necessary work gets done, including the scut work, which thinking people hate.

It is a tall and a paradoxical order.

Hot Potatoes

There are always tasks no one wants to do. They are routine, or unpleasant, or they don't play to our strengths. Paperwork is probably the number one item avoided. Phone calls bother some people. Evaluating people. Filing reports. Getting rid of the old grounds in the coffee pot. Terrible things.

But these tasks still have to be done. And trouble occurs when team members refuse to handle these hot potatoes.

People refuse tasks for different reasons. Their excuses are good ones:

> *"I'm no good at that."*

> *"I did it last year."*

> *"Don't you remember what happened the last time I did that?"*

> *"If you make me do that, we won't be friends any more."*

Managers and team leaders bend over backward to find some way to get these tasks done without forcing team members to do them. They pass them on to resource team members, or farm them out completely to third-party providers. Or they too turn their backs on the unpleasant tasks, and ignore the mounting negatives.

They are wrong to do this. The right thing is to make everyone do their share.

Harvey once overheard a seasoned professional having a wood-shed talk with a raw recruit about what makes a good team member. He was saying, "Ya know, Jake, sometimes ya just gotta suck it up and do things ya don't like."

No one wants to hear that, but it's true. Everyone on a team must pull their fair share of scutwork if the team is to succeed. Exempt some team members, but require it of the others, and you have a two-tier team, which is a no-no.

The scut work in any organization tends to go undone, except by a few people looking for martyr points. These orphaned tasks, roles, or responsibilities pile up and, after a while, start screaming for attention. The emergency nature of these screams takes team members off their measured path and forces them to stamp out the fire.

Like the auto oil filter commercials used to say, "Pay me now, or pay me later." Let unpleasant tasks go unassigned, and thus undone, and you will learn the true meaning of unpleasant.

Good Old Grace

While we are on the subject of hot potatoes, a word about a sickness afflicting some teams.

It is healthy to want to avoid unpleasant tasks. And it is understandable to sigh with relief when someone else gladly takes the assignment on. But beware.

Some people are not so healthy, and faced with an unpleasant task, they will accept it, thinking there is no alternative. These are the passive-nonaggressives—the "zhlubs" of the workplace who do whatever is asked of them, because their self-esteem is so low they can't say no. Most passive-nonaggressives spend their entire lives in this mode, allowing others to very slowly beat them to death. We keep giving them work, and we may even think they like it in some way, because they never complain, except perhaps with a nervous tic.

Good old Grace—you can always count on her!

But here's the problem: Passive-nonaggressiveness is not always stable. One in ten passive-nonaggressives undergoes a change of heart at some point in their lives. They pivot dramatically from passive-nonaggressiveness to the opposite—active-aggressiveness. We call this the Robbins-Finley Flip Switch.

Usually they flip the switch at home, with abusive results. But with teams becoming like another family for many members, the Flip Switch can happen at work as well.

In 1998, 1,400 people were killed in workplace violence. The violence is most often visited upon peers and team members, not on bosses. Risk management statisticians pegged the cost of workplace violence that year at $42 billion. How about that?

Many of the issues in this book, left unaddressed, can lead to this type of tragedy. But the remark police most often elicit from team members run amok is, "I was tired of taking their shit."

Think about that next time you dump weekend work on Grace.

The solution? Be honest as a team. Identify tasks that no one in their right mind wants to do, and rotate them accordingly. Everyone gets a turn at the wheelbarrow.

Turf Wars

Problems also occur when more than one person on a team has responsibility for a single (usually appealing) task. A classic example of this is the senior management team that is not a team at all, because the ambitions of individual members are superseding the team mission. The result: a turf war. Both parties perceive a task as their turf, and they are prepared to violate the spirit of collaboration to ensure the turf remains theirs.

People will fight over just about anything, if they are convinced the turf in question represents power for them, or if they perceive they are painted into a corner. Members of a public relations firm may fight one another to maintain control of an account. Co-leaders of a work team may do battle over who keeps the books, or who has access to the team sponsor. Members of an otherwise purely collaborative effort may come to blows over whose name appears first on the final report.

Both hot potatoes and turf wars spell disaster for team success. Effective teams recognize these potentials, plan for them, and communicate more often when confronted with them.

In the case of hot potatoes, rotating the scut work through all team members (even the most senior) sends a clear message of "pulling your team load." On this team, *everyone* does the dishes. Be careful, however. Perhaps no one wants to take on the hot potato because no one is really qualified to do the task—bookkeeping, say. When there is a genuine gap in team talent, you have to recruit someone else to do the work, if only on a short-term basis.

When turf wars occur, openly negotiate specific tasks. How you communicate content, and how you agree on procedures for updating, linking, collaborating, and accountability are crucial.

Remind people that great teams are cross-functional in design. As in war, team members back one another up. Cross-trained people have primary and secondary roles. If one soldier goes down (with another task, or with the flu), another soldier steps forward and fills in.

Remember to ask this critical question periodically:

Who's responsible for what, by when, and how are we going to check with each other to make sure we're still on track?

chapter 9

The Wrong Policies and Procedures

ne of the responsibilities Harvey had, as a rookie psychologist working for the government, was writing policies and procedures manuals (P&Ps) for groups out in the field.

Ninety-nine times out of 100, his group wrote serious, sober, usable policy books. Every full moon, however, they succumbed to the impulse to create a manual of complete gibberish, full of elliptical provisions that no team in their right mind would follow—mad, foolish, twisted, bureaucratic stuff. And, figuring no one read the books anyway, they sent them out.

Imagine their horror to discover, on field trips many months later, that these policy and procedure manuals were being treated as though they had been handed down from Mt. Sinai on stone tablets. People actually went out of their way to try and make the absurd nostrums work, wasting time and productivity along the way.

Harvey was not only ashamed that he had had a hand in contributing to the delinquency of our government, but he was angry at the lemmings who blindly followed the obviously idiotic policies he had scripted.

What We Have Learned

The lesson of this shameful episode—Harvey still bursts into tears at odd intervals, just thinking about it—is that some balance has to be found in the area of policies and procedures.

Organizations and teams themselves must create policies and procedures that are credible. Credibility means that the information in the P&Ps, those vast and weighty tomes stashed in the credenza, must parallel reality.

Too many companies and too many teams live a double life—their life by the book and their real life. When the book and reality diverge too sharply, they acquire separate lives. People who perform well in the actual organization go with the flow of the organization; people who perform better "by the book" will cling to it, chapter and verse, stifling their own growth and creativity.

Those who snicker at policies and procedures manuals are really snickering at their corporate culture. The company may say these binders describe the company—but people know better. Their organization, and they themselves, are living a lie. The gap between the credenza and real life is too great. Bad rules have a corrosive effect on the bond holding teams and entire enterprises together.

In business after business, we see the same thing happening: people blindly following P&Ps that may have been relevant at one time, but are now clearly outdated. It may take the form of new product introduction steps ("You must follow all 19 steps"), procedures for the procurement of products or services—even elaborate, trademarked models for the corporate decision-making process, that all decision makers at all levels are supposed to follow.

Manuals become the fiefdom of certain, otherwise powerless, centralized departments, like Personnel. These departments occasionally make a religion out of the big book, because it is all they have. Sections are individually dated, amendments are marked, reprints are shipped out once a month—at times one wonders if the true purpose of the organization isn't just to maintain up-to-date policy manuals.

Mike once served as a corporate director of communications. The first day on the job, he was escorted to his new digs. He was shown his desk, his phone, his in-box—and then, with a flourish, he was shown the office credenza. It was a black cabinet about five feet wide. Its three shelves were piled deep with successive versions of the company's employee manuals—at least 60 three-ring notebooks, each page of each book noting its date of publication and the page number it was superseding. "These notebooks are our past, our present, and our future," his superior said. "Respect them."

Mike stared at the credenza, open-mouthed. What had he got himself into? In retrospect, it would have done that organization a world of good to heap all those manuals into a pile and light up the western sky with them. Manuals are "paper supervisors," a holdover from the preteam era. Do we still need them at all?

Some kind of on-paper guide to corporate life is necessary. We believe a proper manual should include the basic things team members and other workers need to know about working at a company: its mission, what is expected of employees, and what is promised in return by the organization as a whole. If there is a chain of command, workers need to know what it is. If there are procedures for filing grievances, that is necessary information.

But for heaven's sake, try and keep the manual short. "Manual," after all, implies it should be liftable with a single hand; many of these three-ring P&P Frankensteins require a fork lift to raise off the ground.

Make sure that any P&Ps teams are asked to abide by are relevant and timely. We suggest that teams put expiration dates on policies, just like medicine. On the expiration date, policies are reexamined for relevance. If not relevant, they are flushed, like old penicillin. If they still make sense, the policy prescription is refilled. After all, eggs and milk have expiration dates, so why not have them for things that really go stale, like organizational rules?

In addition, during the sanity checking of P&Ps, good teams take a stab at identifying barriers (people, processes, structures) that may be getting in the way of achieving desired outcomes. They continuously identify and strategize ways around these barriers as a regular way of doing team business.

There is nothing wrong with the idea of policies and procedures. But they should be guidelines, helpful ideas to turn to in time of doubt—not a needle's eye to squeeze the actual corporation through. Ideally, we should see them as snapshots that fade over time. Instead, we have paper Stonehenges that never go away.

At the bottom of every page in the binder you'll see one of two dates. There's the "effective" date, which is often something from the twilight of corporate time, like 1/1/68. And there's the "revision" date, something only a little less antediluvian, like 9/30/72. Now we are proposing a third date—the "expiration" date. After 1/1/2002, the idea goes bye-bye, unless consciously reimbued with life. Every idea, every policy, every procedure, should be reviewed every two to three years. Modify and extend those that deserve it, and deep-six the remainder—particularly if you notice team members systematically going around a procedure to do their jobs, a sure sign of a procedure that should not be.

Remember that it's easier to ask for forgiveness than for permission. More good things happen when you are willing to bend the rules.

Sometimes, of course, the perfect solution for too many rules is a nice roaring fire. This is essentially what happened in the two big American car success stories of the last decade, Ford Taurus and GM Saturn. Ford and GM looked at the baseline, decided it was too screwed-up to build upon, and so built entirely new divisions, making a fresh, honest start in the policies and procedures area. The fresh start gave both of these "skunkworks" projects terrific vitality, and a head start toward success.

Policies and procedures are supposed to serve the team, not the other way around.

chapter 10

The People Problem

When we think about teams, we tend to picture the perfect team. Its members are autonomous, intelligent, generous-minded, and quick to fill in where others leave off. The members of this perfect team fall somewhere between angels and the characters sketched in apparel ads.

You need to take this mental picture of the perfect team, fold it into careful squares, set it on a platform, and blow it to smithereens. Because you may live to be 108, but you will never be on anything remotely like a perfect team.

Ideal teams are comprised of perfect people, whose egos and individuality have been subsumed into the greater goal of the team. Real teams—your teams—are made up of living, breathing, and very imperfect people. Even when you personally handpick a team, it is still likely to contain people that you (or other team members) will be really challenged to get along with.

Our experience is that, in the forming stage especially, nearly all team members are taken aback by the personalities of other team members: X is an asocial jerk, Y is borderline psychotic, and Z is a shameless jackass.

That's what we have to work with on teams, and that is a major, major reason teams fail.

But mostly, we are just different enough to create misunderstandings. These can be overcome, but they require self-knowledge, generous attention to the person who's bugging us, and the will to keep working together, and to not give up on one another.

We tend to give up on one another too easily, to write off poor working relationships as "personality incompatibilities." Most of these incompatibilities can be resolved with a bit of empathy and attention.

Sometimes we are so different from one another, and so poisonous to one another, that there is no hope for the team. That's what our next chapter is about.

For now, let's look at what is achievable. It means moving beyond first impressions and stereotypes, beyond expectations of apparel-ad perfection, and into the muck and mire of what it is to be human beings in all our diverse, peculiar glory—and how to tolerate those who are not as marvelous as ourselves.

The Logic of Misunderstanding

Even the best teams suffer continuous setbacks because of simple misunderstandings. What we intend to communicate (what we transmit) is seldom exactly what we succeed in communicating (what the other party receives).

Why does this happen? In a word, diversity. We all have different minds, different slants, different hot buttons. We come from different cultures, both ethnic and familial. We share different histories. We have different brains inside our heads.

When the message transmitted is not the message received, the result is not usually obvious catastrophe. It is more like a plane that is subtly out of control. It won't crash; it will stay in the air. People on the plane will think they are succeeding, because miles are rolling by on the odometer. Passengers stare out the windows, maybe even waving, confident they are en route to their destination, even as they fly farther and farther off course.

Every year we flush billions of dollars through our organizations, sunk costs caused by the kinds of everyday misunderstandings and ambiguities we all participate in. You have seen the sign over the photocopy machine:

"I know you think you understand what you thought I said. But I am not sure that what you heard is what I meant."

The worst part of this incredible waste is that we learn next to nothing from it. In our minds it is always the other person's fault for mistransmitting or misreceiving. In reality, there is no fault in a classic miscommunication.

Misunderstandings often occur for the simple reason that the individuals involved are communicating on two different wavelengths. How you communicate with others is influenced to a very large degree by what kind of person you are—by your "behavioral style." Preventing miscommunication means being very alert to your own behavioral style, as well as to the style of the person you are talking to. It requires that we relearn how to communicate with others in a way that is cognizant of their differing natures and sensitive to their needs.

Happy Talk and Human Variation

As we have noted, the picture-perfect team seen in magazine articles doesn't exist. Indeed, the cheerful attitude that typifies books, articles, and presentations about teams is misleading. Teams cannot solve all your organization's problems. Nothing can.

The horrible truth is that the people on your teams will be like people everywhere. They may be smart in one or two areas, but normal or below normal in other ways—ways that have a bearing on your team success. Team members have their ups and downs. You will have team members who are clinically depressed, or who have serious personality disorders. You will have team members you just can't stand.

You will have team members who might once have been terrific contributors, but whose brains have lost efficiency. Their neuro-transmitters don't fire with the rapidity or regularity that they did fifteen years earlier, or before they were damaged by alcohol, or an accident, or the passage of time.

You will go home thinking you have the greatest team in the world, and find out the next morning that one of your stars has been arrested, or is dead. You will have team members whose judgment varies widely from day to day—a sage on Monday, a fool on Tuesday.

These are depressing realities. We say them not to discourage you, but to remind you that your on-the-job team problems are just a slice of the problems of life itself.

The happy-talk articles won't tell you that. We just did.

People are not the same. They are as different as thumbprints—and not just in one way, such as preferring white or dark turkey meat, or being vegetarian. People are different up and down, through and through, coming and going—in their likes, dislikes, fears, joys, the ways they think and decide, the ways they work and communicate.

Teams succeed when they acknowledge this fact of natural variation, and work to recognize and value differences among team members.

It often happens, when we start talking about different personality types, that some cheerful HR person will suggest the Myers-Briggs Type Inventory (MBTI) as a tool. The MBTI tells you how you see yourself, and gives you a set of label initials to wear through life (ISTJ, ENSP, etc.). It has become a kind of psychological parlor game. Lots of people have taken the test, and the initials they receive help them understand themselves, and forgive people born with different characteristics. It is a very interesting system, especially valuable for the task of self-discovery.

But how you see yourself or how you really are inside doesn't matter much to teams. How you behave on the outside, how you treat other people and how you demand to be treated, is what matters. Teams have enough to handle without taking on spiritual adjustments. But team behavior is fair game. Reduce miscommunication, straighten out confusing behavior, and get people working together more effectively—that you can do.

In the work world, we could generally give two hoots what a person's insides are like. That is their business, after all. But how they act—and interact—is essential to their value to the enterprise. You don't have to like one another to produce together. You do have to "get along."

Denver psychologist David Merril, of the TRACOM training firm, describes people as falling into four approximate behavioral profiles or zones. It is a very handy way to think about behavioral differences. One of these four behavior zones is, for you, a kind of "home plate"—a place which, day in and day out, other people see you as occupying. The four home plates together make up a big square, like this:

ANALYTICAL	DRIVER
Key Value: Work with existing circumstances to promote quality in products and services	**Key Value:** Shape the environment by overcoming opposition to get immediate results
Orientation: Thinking	**Orientation:** Action
Time: Past	**Time:** Present
AMIABLE	EXPRESSIVE
Key Value: Cooperate with others, make sure people are included and feel good about the process	**Key Value:** Shape the environment by bringing others into alliance to generate enthusiasm for the results
Orientation: Relationships	**Orientation:** Intuition
Time: Depends on who they are with at the time	**Time:** Future

Think of the diagram as one way of looking at the universe of human personality, with a distinct north, south, east, and west. From right to left it measures assertiveness, from passivity to activity, or from "asking" to "telling." From top to bottom it measures responsiveness, whether we react in a controlled fashion (top) or in an emotional fashion (bottom).

Thus a "Driver" is a combination of task-oriented and proactive. An "Expressive" is a combination of proactive and people-oriented. An "Amiable" is people-oriented and reactive, and an "Analytical" is a combination of reactive and task-oriented.*

As we paint a mental picture of each of the four types, be thinking about which type people see you as.

▶ *Analyticals* are essentially perfectionists, people who serve no wine, take no precipitous action, before its time. The very best thing about Analyticals is that, nine times out of ten, they are right about things, because they gave the matter their time, reflection, and rational consideration. Their strong suit is the facts. Their key virtue is patience, and it may also be their downfall—a kind of caution that paralyzes, not from fear but from a determination to fully understand a problem before moving toward a solution. Pushed to the brink, the response of the Analytical is usually to run for cover until the shooting stops.

Adjectives that are sometimes attached to Analyticals: *critical, indecisive, stuffy, picky, moralistic, industrious, persistent, serious, expecting, orderly.*

▶ *Amiables* are essentially "people people," considerate of other people, and very empathic. They are the "warm fuzzies" of the world. Their orientation is the past, the present and the future— wherever people have needs, and may be hurt. They are the world's best coordinators, precisely because they take time to

---

* For the record, Harvey is an Amiable with a strong Expressive dimension, and Mike is an Expressive with a murky Analytical element.

touch base with all parties. Sure, they have opinions—but they may be more interested to know yours. Their great strength is their understanding of relationships. Pushed to the brink, their response is usually to cave in.

Adjectives that are sometimes attached to Amiables: *conforming, unsure, ingratiating, dependent, awkward, supportive, respectful, willing, dependable, agreeable.*

▶ *Drivers* are essentially let-me-do-it people. They are firmly rooted in the present moment, and they are lovers of action. Their great strength: results. If you want a job discussed, talk to one of the other three types; if you just want it done, take it to a Driver. They aren't much for inner exploration, but they sure bring home the bacon. They can be bitterly self-critical, and resentful of idle chit-chat. Favorite song: "Steamroller Blues." Pushed to the brink, Drivers become tyrants.

Adjectives that are sometimes attached to Drivers: *pushy, severe, tough, dominating, harsh, strong-willed, independent, practical, decisive, efficient.*

▶ *Expressives* are essentially big-picture people, always looking for a fresh perspective on the world around them. They are future-oriented, perhaps because that is where no one can ever pin them down as they dream their grand dreams. If you want a straight answer, Expressives may not be the best place to turn. If you want intuition and creativity, they're wonderful. If you want a terrific party, invite lots of Expressives. Pushed to the brink, Expressives can react savagely, by attacking. Though cheerful nine ways out of ten, they take the world they create in their heads very seriously.

Adjectives that are sometimes attached to Expressives: *manipulating, excitable, undisciplined, reacting, egotistical, ambitious, stimulating, wacky, enthusiastic, dramatic, friendly.*

Now, on teams we are likely to find all these behavioral types mixed together, and expected to communicate with each other. This is not an irrational expectation—we are all carbon-based lifeforms, we are all featherless bipeds, and we mostly speak the same language.

But come on—putting an Analytical in the same room with an Expressive? A Driver with an Amiable? A Driver with an Expressive? Imagine a dinner party featuring:

▶ irrepressible comic Roberto Benini

▶ humble, serious, pious Mother Teresa

▶ sassy, snappish Judge Judy

▶ introverted but confident Bill Gates

▶ flamboyant hip-hopper Puff Daddy Combs

▶ owlish intellectual George Will

You know, with a mix like this, there will be a few breaks in the conversation. The six may admire each other to death, but finding common ground will be a challenge. Just imagine how George Will might suffer sitting next to Roberto Benini at meetings. Or the look on Bill Gates' face as Judge Judy's gavel comes down on him.

Well, that is what most teams are like—odd assemblies of mismatched personalities. Chances are excellent that your teams are experiencing real communication problems.

We can't solve all the complex communications snafus your entire team is experiencing, but here are some ideas on how you can straighten out your own communications with the others.

First, identify your communication style. Do you come across to others as an Analytical, an Amiable, a Driver, or an Expressive? Probably you accept one of the four designations, but reluctantly, because of the negatives associated with each.

Second, adapt your style to suit the needs of whoever you're communicating with.

Can you change your style? Yes and no. To go from being one style to its opposite—from a pure Analytical to a pure Expressive—would probably make your head explode. But you can soften the extremeness of your style, and learn how to communicate with people in other styles.

Here are some tips to help you make the empathic crossing to each of the four styles.

With Drivers, strive to:

▶ Be brief and to the point. Think "efficiency."

▶ Stick to business. Skip the chit-chat. Close loopholes. Dispel ambiguities. Digress at your peril. Speculate and you're history.

▶ Be prepared. Know the requirements and objectives of the task at hand.

▶ Organize your arguments into a neat "package." Present your facts cleanly and logically.

▶ Be courteous, not chummy. Don't be bossy; drivers do not let themselves be driven.

▶ Ask specific questions. Don't go "fishing" for answers.

▶ If you disagree, disagree with the facts, not the person.

▶ If you agree, support the results and the person.

▶ Persuade by citing objectives and results. Outcomes rule!

▶ When finished, leave. No loitering.

With Expressives, strive to:

▶ Meet their social needs while talking shop. Entertain, stimulate, be lively.

▶ Talk about their goals as well as the team's.

▶ Be open—strong and silent does not cut it with Expressives.

▶ Take time. They are most efficient when not in a hurry.

▶ Ask for their opinions and ideas.

▶ Keep your eye on the big picture, not the technical details.

▶ Support your points with examples involving people they know and respect.

▶ Offer special deals, extras, and incentives.

▶ Show honest respect; you must not talk down to an Expressive.

With Amiables, strive to:

▶ Break the ice—it shows your commitment to the task and to them.

▶ Show respect. Amiables will be hurt by any attempt to patronize.

▶ Listen and be responsive. Take your time. Learn the whole story.

▶ Be nonthreatening, casual, informal. A crisp, commanding style will send Amiables packing.

▶ Ask "how" questions to draw out their opinions.

▶ Define what you want them to contribute to the task.

▶ Assure and guarantee that the decision at hand will in no way risk, harm, or threaten others. But make no assurances you can't back up.

With Analyticals, strive to:

▶ Prepare your case in advance.

▶ Take your time, but be persistent.

▶ Support their principles. Show you value their thoughtful approach.

▶ Cover all bases. Do not leave things to chance, or hope "something good will happen."

▶ Draw up a scheduled approach for any action plan. Be specific on roles and responsibilities.

▶ Be clear. Disorganization or sloppiness in presentation is a definite turn-off.

▶ Avoid emotional arguments. No wheedling or cajoling. No pep rallies.

▶ Follow through. The worst thing you can do with Analyticals is break your word, because they will remember.

Let's Think

What we are urging, with all this talk about personality types, is not that you be a chameleon, changing your colors to match the colors of the people you are dealing with. Rather, we suggest you try to see things through their eyes, and understand their needs and preferences.

It is critical for people with weaknesses in one area—such as visionary people who tend to go limp in the nuts-and-bolts department—to either delegate authority or to redouble their efforts to think practically. It is equally critical, in ordinary communication, for one type to know what another type is listening for.

You are not a rat in a box, that can make only one response to every stimulus. You are a human being, with a host of choices in every situation.

We are urging that you choose to be curious about other people's natures and needs and accommodate them when possible. When you do this, you will find them accommodating you in return. This reciprocal accommodation is just another dimension of teamwork.

Let's Play

One problem we sometimes encounter, as we lay out our little grid of human nature, is that people think the entire universe of human nature is somewhere in there. Which means they must be in there, somewhere. But it's just a two-dimensional model, showing how two important traits, Assertiveness and Responsiveness, reveal our diversity.

Now imagine that you could take these four squares and make them cubes—by adding a third dimension, one coming toward you. Call it Direction, and let it measure the inwardness/outwardness, or introversion/extroversion of personality. Do this and the true complexity of personality becomes visible.

The two-dimensional Driver might be a cardboard cutout of Boy Scout values. But there is no law saying Drivers can't also be introverts—leaders by nature, but not sharers. Instead of driving you, they drive themselves. It's not necessarily a good combination—these are leaders prone to workplace illnesses, migraines, workaholism, and high gastrointestinal awareness.

Then there's the introverted Expressives. You may see them coming down the hall, smiling, whistling a tune, high as a kite. Inside they're having a party—but no one else is invited to it.

Or you might have extroverted Analyticals, as opposed to the stereotypical introverted nerds. These are the people who chase you down the hall quoting facts, figures, reasons, and contraindications. They're being 100 percent social with matters most people don't consider social fodder.

You will dread the extroverted Amiables—they want to be with you so much they make you want to move to another state.

Well, guess what—that's the 3-D world of team personality. Full of complexity, ambiguity, contradiction, and surprises.

Let's Work

Now let's subject the model to the acid test. Does it work across racial, gender, and ethnic lines?

Yes, yes, and no.

In any given culture, men and women, and people of different races, are as likely to be in one square as another. Men aren't the only Drivers, nor are women the only Amiables—not by a long shot. It's the same with races.

But travel from culture to culture, and changes occur. What happens is that the grid is no longer big enough. Some groups are literally "off the chart" in some categories.

This is something we did not fully appreciate when we wrote the first edition of this book. But traveling from country to country, and seeing how teams broke down in different places, we became convinced that some groups occupy psychological ground, in the aggregate, that other groups can hardly conceptualize.

If we were to draw the box in Pacific Rim cultures, for instance, we would want to move the entire box one click to the left, to accommodate a remarkable potential for analysis and an aversion to individual panache. What looks like an Analytical idea to us, to them would be considered evidence of leadership—the realm we associate with Drivers. Their idea of "charisma" is far steelier and reserved than the American idea. Their business timelines—50-year business plans are common in Hong Kong and Japan, and even 100-year business plans exist—make Americans resemble hummingbirds in constancy. And they embody a talent for collaborative work that is the envy of every other team culture. On the superficial level, this insight accounts for ethnic stereotypes—Germans responding well to order and leadership, the Japanese adoring anything to do with teams.

Draw a box for Europe, and the box shifts in the opposite direction—one click to the right. In that flamboyant realm, the person an American would regard as a Driver is regarded as a mere Analytical! In reserved Scandinavia, the model shifts a click to the north. In passionate Latin America, one click to the south.

We stress that people are not so different from continent to continent as to be incomprehensible to one another. Just that "one click's worth" of difference can often be enough to confound and put cultures off from another.

In a global economy, and belonging to global teams, we ignore these cultural strengths and weaknesses at our peril.

The Will to Team

Most personalities, we conclude, fall within the normal range, and can be dealt with if we simply acknowledge our differences and learn what we all want from one another. Once we get that out of the way, we can go to work and earn some money.

When you start to know people, it's easier to root for them. We want the team to succeed not just for the team's sake, but for everyone's sake. That's the foundation of team spirit right there—learning combined with the willingness to act upon what we learn.

This *will to team* doesn't sound like much, but it's critical to team success. Without it, all the training, rewards and recognitions, meetings, pronouncements, consultants, weekend retreats, etc. are worthless. No team can be a team against its will.

Teams achieve this "willing" state only one way—by learning about one another and by caring. Both must occur. Where there is no learning, no knowledge, no information, there can be no caring. But if people have made up their minds not to give a damn, neither can there be any learning.

So shape up out there, all you teams. You don't have to like one another especially. But you do have to get to know one another, and to value one another's abilities and individuality. Meet teammates halfway with your respect and understanding, and together you can move the team objectives forward.

chapter 11

Dealing with Difficult People

owhere is it written that you have to get along with everyone. There are people in the world who should not, who must not, be on any team—ever. And they are not especially unusual.

In the last chapter we talked about people whose intentions toward teaming were OK, but whose ability to team successfully was hampered by differences of opinion and approach. This chapter is about people who nature did not inculcate with the instinct or the will to team.

They are not necessarily bad people, although some (the dark angels) *are* truly bad. All require action on the team's part—either distancing, discipline, or banishment.

Team Jerks

On any given day, we can all be jerks—rude people unaware of how we come across. But the true team jerk goes beyond occasional jerkness to full-blown jerkhood. They are jerks par excellence. Compared to them, we are amateurs.

A team jerk is usually its most talented member. He or she may have made some very important contributions to the enterprise.

Their specialty is ideas—new technologies, new products, new processes, new applications, new combinations of existing things, new marketing ideas. Extraordinarily bright and creative, they are high-achieving dynamos when motivated, giving off ideas the way regular folk emit carbon dioxide.

Take Bert (please!). He is a prima donna about his talent. He won't play by the rules other team members follow. He demands that other people attend to him, while he ignores them. Communication with him has eroded to the point where the team simply ignores him—while hoping he includes them the next time a great idea comes to him. When team members do try to include him in things, he brushes them off.

A good archetype for Bert is the software programmer who is a genius with C++, but has horrendous social skills. You hate to lose his talent, but you could sure do without his arrogance, his eccentricities, and his contempt. (Wouldn't hurt if he bathed a bit more often, either.)

What can you do with a guy like Bert?

First, acknowledge that his personality is not his fault. None of us asks to be born with the precise set of talents and peculiarities we get. The jerk is often blessed with great creativity, but cursed with a crummy personality.

There are two strong opposing forces in the creative person. One force arises from internal standards, which are precious and, in many ways, the secret to that person's success. At all costs, the creative jerk admits, one must be true to that inner measure. The other force is something we are more familiar with—the drive we all have for recognition by others. The problem is that the two forces don't reconcile all that easily. Especially bright people have to struggle to know which drive to honor at any given moment.

Second, appreciate that what you see is probably not all there is. People who seem arrogant often have profound insecurities. People who laugh in your face may well cry when you are gone. These people may simply be failing to adequately communicate what is going on inside them. The sad secret of many creative types is that they are experiencing more stress and more pain than other team members.

In addition, an individual who is susceptible to the terrible pressures of the workplace is probably not immune to pressures on the home front, either. It's possible that behind the superficial inappropriate behavior may lurk problems far more difficult to solve—marital conflicts, chemical abuse, even mental illness. Historically, creative geniuses have always had a knack for turning their right-brain talents against themselves.

Third, see if the team itself is helping to create the problem. Maybe team members have unconsciously "outed" the jerk because he is cut from such a different bolt of cloth than they are. Or maybe the team rules and policies are too narrow to accommodate a personality with extra, um, verve.

Having made these adaptations, however, you still have the problem of Bert being Bert. You can change the whole world to suit some people, and they will continue to be jerks.

Here's a radical idea: Why not ask him what he would like? Ask if he wants to continue as a team member. Ask him if there is anything he would like done differently—whom to report to, how and how often to meet, whether to work side by side or from remote locations. Make clear that you are searching for a solution that enables him to keep being himself, doing the quality of work he does, and making some kind of contribution to the team—and that alleviates the personality clashes that are making everyone miserable.

If he perceives himself to be at war with the team, he may be very wary of such a pow-wow. So you must be very supportive, yet very candid with him.

The best solution may be to put some distance between him and the team. Set him apart from the core team, as a valued resource team member. Make him a unit unto himself—a team of one—with a dotted-line relationship to the team, as a reference source, sounding board, or technology guru. Set him up as a one-man skunkworks. Give him an office in a separate building, or on a separate continent, even. Buy him some bunny slippers and make a telecommuter out of him.

Be careful about sending your genius off to the jungle by himself, however. The idea of separation may sound good to both him and to the team, but it may backfire. It's very likely that Bert needs human contact to keep from going completely insane, or from becoming depressed. The team he derides and ignores may be his lifeline.

Perhaps the best solution is for the team to accept the fact that it needs Bert and Bert, though he gives little indication of this, needs the team. Why not make a concerted effort to give Bert what he needs—admiration, support, and sympathy? Just because he doesn't act especially human doesn't mean he is immune to human feelings. We all need a kind word from time to time, and the occasional reassuring pat on the back.

Now that you have his attention, let your newfound appreciation be the basis on which a new alliance can be built between the problem individual and you. Once he sees you are a true fan, you can do something. Acknowledge his talents, but put an arm around his shoulder and say, "Hey, if we're going to let that talent blossom, we have to do something about these self-defeating behaviors."

Don't apply the medicine, the behavioral change, until you have first proffered the candy of encouragement and fellow-feeling.

And when the time comes to name those self-defeating obnoxious behaviors, be specific. It's no good using value-laden, broad-brush terms like *jerk, arrogant, obtuse son-of-a-bitch,* etc.

Instead, say:

"It appears to me that you shoot from the hip during the meetings, and you hurt people's feelings and make enemies."

"It appears to me that you can't take criticism. When I asked you about your design at Thursday's meeting, you got up and left the room."

"It seems as if you like making cruel jokes, and you don't know how badly that makes people feel."

"Julie, the transcriptionist, quit because you yelled at her."

"I left six messages on your voicemail and you never got back to me."

"You play Cubanismo! *when the rest of us are trying to read professional journals."*

The creative high-achiever has a hot pilot light. He or she burns hotter and works harder than most people. And where all of us have an inner core into which we descend from time to time in our lives, the creative high-achiever virtually camps out there, intensely focused on whatever it is he or she is striving to create or achieve. They are almost of a different race from the rest of us—we are turtles and they are racehorses. Small wonder if adapting to our hobbling pace causes them problems.

One thing about them is that you can't help them by slowing them down. Stress for them may actually be lower when their activity level is hyper or beyond. Never tell a racehorse to walk a few laps. Creatives and high achievers are often subspecies of workaholics, and workaholics have a way of dying within a year of retirement.

Can people, whether they are genius-jerks or whatever, really get hold of their basic natures and change them? How many teams have ever witnessed the kind of transformation necessary to turn around a career?

And even when the results are good, the process may not be over. A team member who has alienated everyone on the team will find that his transformation is not universally trusted. Like the boy who cried wolf too often, the genius-no-longer-(such)-a-jerk will find that many colleagues are hard to win over. There is a degree to which people almost prefer the two-dimensionality of poor behavior to the unpredictability of more sensitive behavior. So sometimes more has to change than just the individual. Sometimes the team has to change as well.

Team Blowhards

In the old Aesop fairy tale, one thing stood between a houseful of mice and complete happiness—the cat. So the mice met and voted to eliminate the danger forever, by tying a bell around the cat's neck. With the bell in place, the cat would be unable to sneak up on and devour another mouse. The only problem was getting volunteers to tie the bell on.

The same goes with teams. Nearly every team has one member, either a leader or a peer, who cannot seem to help dominating team activities. Even when time is short, and the agenda is crowded, these blowhards feel they have to get their share of attention. Team blowhards talk too often, too long, are impossible to shut up, enjoy initiating distractions, and just generally dominate team proceedings.

What can the team do to suppress these people? Putting a bell on them doesn't work—we saw it tried once, and, well, the blowhards just take it off. But there are other solutions.

The most conventional solutions are managerial in nature. They are old-fashioned, autocratic, preteam remedies by which the team leader shuts up the noisy and encourages the quiet. The most drastic is to simply terminate the overbearing offender. Termination may seem like the perfect weapon in all kinds of team personality issues, but beware. Termination:

▶ is unfair; you're effectively dismissing someone for over-contributing.

▶ is potentially litigious; nothing like a team lawsuit to bring folks together.

▶ subtly undermines the authority of the team leader; it shows you can't manage a simple situation.

▶ is inefficient; you have thrown out the baby with the bathwater, wasted a whole team member to eliminate a single flaw.

Some teams "quarantine" overbearing members; they redesignate them as wing units to get them out of the office. But here again, keeping expressive people at home—banning them from the regular environment—wastes talent. Meanwhile, it's nearly always a bad idea to change a job description to suit an individual.

In meetings, some team leaders bell the bully by artificially ostracizing him from the team process, by assigning him the task of flipping the flipcharts, or manning the light switch at the back of the room. If a bully is talking, it is possible to talk through them—the inappropriate sound of two voices vying for attention gets even the biggest bully's attention.

Some team leaders turn their backs to the overtalker—you don't reinforce what you don't see. You can simply ignore them. If they are constantly raising hands, don't look their way. If they interrupt, smile and say, "Let's look at that later."

Call on other team members to help. "Come on, gang, let's not let Audrey here do all the work. Who else has an idea? Who agrees with Audrey? Disagrees?"

If the bully seems unmoved by all these attempts, take her or him aside during a break and say in no uncertain terms: "You are dragging the group away from the agenda. If you keep this up, the team will be a joke. If you can't adjust to the agenda, you're not welcome here."

The most important tool in combating distraction is the team agenda. Make your agenda central, and stick to it at all costs. If someone goes off on a tangent, pull them back. An agenda keeps you from being the "bad person." You say, "George that is really very interesting, but it is not what we agreed to discuss today." Let the agenda take the heat for disciplining the process. You're not disagreeing—you're just keeping things on track.

If someone is dominating, they still have to breathe. When they stop for that breath, leap in, and say, "George, that's interesting—can we relate that back to the agenda before us?" You can also simply say, "George that's interesting, but let me hear from other people, too." And then you turn your eye contact away and poll others for opinions.

Some team leaders take preemptive action, heading the bully off at the pass before he or she ruins the team. The more you can do before a team get-together, hammering out an understanding of the tasks at hand, the better the meeting will go. Likewise, there are post-meeting strategies to ensure meeting success. He who controls the minutes controls the meeting.

There are social solutions to the problem of blowhards—ways of communicating that overtalkers need to turn it down, and undertalkers need to summon the courage to speak. Consider throwing the bully a bone. People who want attention can sometimes be satisfied—or frightened away—with a little. Say, "Good idea, Jack. Anybody else?" It doesn't have to be a big bone. But never appease a bully with flattery ("Roy, you have so many wonderful ideas!"). Positive reinforcement only invites more of the reinforced behavior.

The worst person to have on a team is the negative thinker. "We tried that, and it didn't work," is this person's bludgeon. One tactic is to turn that person's negativity around: "How would you make it work this time?" "How can we overcome those obstacles?"

The imbalance between shy people and demonstrative people can be a major problem for team interaction. How do you achieve the team ideal—everyone participating, everyone contributing—if one person drowns out the others? A skilled team manager knows how to keep from being steamrolled by compulsive hard-driving Type A behavior, by authoritarian personalities who think it is fitting and natural that others should obey them, and by "Machiavellian manipulators," people on the lookout for a neck to sharpen their axe on—yours.

Throw in the cultural and attitudinal deference often given to males, to people with booming voices, to tall people, and the natural advantage of seniority on the company flow chart, and there is a lot to overcome.

Team leaders need to plan solutions to these problems in advance. Structure the information so that people know, when the team meeting starts, what is expected of them, what is permitted, and what is out of line. Announce that you want everyone's input, not just one or two people's. With that understanding in mind, individuals are less likely to hijack the team.

Challenge them to prove that their point of view is substantive, that they have something relevant to say, and are not just talking to hear their tongues flap. Look them dead in the eye and ask them, "If you could make your point in 25 words, what would it be?"

Try to win them to your side. "I like what you are saying, but I have only a short time to make my points here—could I go first?" If necessary, shut the blowhard down. "I have no idea what the answer to the question of parking privileges is. I'm here to talk about the team's strategy."

One strategy is to "equalize" group membership through something called the nominal group technique. Here the facilitator asks group members to quietly write down what their thoughts are on the coming meeting. Then the facilitator reads the ideas, thus controlling group input. This approach can be linked with electronic meeting tools, which we will discuss in a later chapter.

Team Brats

Judith Bardwick, in her book *Danger in the Comfort Zone* (New York: Amacom, 1991), describes an attitude that has crept gradually into the workplace in recent years—one that spells unavoidable death to successful teaming. She calls the attitude "entitlement." It is a team member's feeling that the rest of the team, or the organization as a whole, owes him or her membership. If entitlement is too abstract a phrase, consider the one your parents used when you acted like that at age five—spoiled brat.

In the old days there was no spoiled brat syndrome because no organization spoiled its workers, except for the few lucky ones at the top. But in our century there has slowly evolved a belief—and it is shared by many nations and many systems, from capitalism to communism—that people have an inherent right to fair treatment, a living wage, and decent conditions.

That doesn't sound too bad. In fact, you probably want to agree that those things should be guaranteed to all people. The problem is that as these assumptions have evolved, they have become sloppy, and people—human nature being what it is—have taken advantage. Lots of people in lots of organizations decided that the new contract between organizations and team members should put the entire onus for doing on the organization, and none on the team member.

People are too often too comfortable and held to too little account. And for years, people have been succeeding as individuals, without necessarily contributing to the success of their teams.

Brattism says: "I have what I have because the team owes it to me. I get it simply by existing, not by doing." Spoiled Brat Syndrome happens at every level. It is the CEO holding out for a $5 million bonus and a golden parachute compensation plan, despite unprofitability for investors and ruthless downsizing for workers. It is the shortsighted investor, only interested in what an investment nets for him, not in what the business makes or does. It is the perks and plush carpets of Congressional offices during budgetary cutbacks. It is unions demanding 95 percent of salary for workers when they are not working.

At the team level, brattism is team members waiting for someone else to show leadership, to volunteer, to share information, to take chances. It is people hiding behind functions ("I'm in marketing, you need to talk to sales"). It is complaining about compensation when the team has not produced anything worthwhile for the organization. It is teams with poorly formed objectives and goals performing pointless tasks they know have no value or utility, all the while insisting they are burning the midnight oil.

The terrible irony is that the utopian idea of providing a more secure life for workers has too often undermined the American Dream. Brattism is a primary cause of bloat, bureaucracy, turf wars, indifferent service, and shoddy product quality.

It is also the cause of a shift in our character and our ethics, a point Bardwick made in her book. When we are not held to account for our actions, it is easy to rationalize our shortcomings:

No one else is working hard, so why should I? If no one catches you, you didn't do anything wrong. A job not worth doing is not worth doing well.

How does a team combat incipient brattism? Through vigilance and intolerance. By keeping the team on track to achieve their stated objectives, and by making sure those objectives are actually achievable.

Team members slip into brattism for two main reasons: the team's objectives are unachievable, or they are too easily achieved. Teams require just the right degree of engagement, or members rebel and drift into defiant antiteam attitudes.

Restoring a team from brattism to honest engagement doesn't happen without leadership. The first order for leaders is to clear away any vestige of brattism at the top. No team is going to come clean and shed its bad attitudes while the team at the top is permitted to continue with its own.

The leader then administers pressure. Either people perform, or they depart. But the pressure must be to achieve a very specific outcome. Rewards must be for achievements that matter, not for digging and refilling holes. But people must feel their work is important. People who cannot make the crossing to be more accountable even with training must be winnowed out and replaced.

The passage from an attitude of brattism to being a working member of a team is not an easy one. It requires pain and anxiety, by definition. Brattism is like dope that numbs us to the twinges of reality. But at the end of this anxious journey is the possibility of great success and great fulfillment. The feeling of achieving this success makes the aches and pains worthwhile.

Dark Angels

There are people out there who should not be on any team, anywhere, ever. We are not referring to reclusives or the terminally shy. They can participate. We are talking about the organizational equivalent of the undead. If you follow the medical model, you would say they are sociopathic. If you are a strict moralist, you will call them evil. If you lean more toward the supernatural, you might call them dark angels.

A dark angel can take several forms:

▶ *the addict,* who acts crazy because of some personal problem

▶ *the ogre,* who acts out of antisocial rage

▶ *the crook,* who thinks nothing of crossing ethical lines

▶ *the fanatic,* who puts achieving his objectives above all rules and policies

Here's what a dark angel can do.

A team of five was set up to study the feasibility of direct marketing a new product. Everyone on the team seemed to have a reasonable amount of team spirit, except for Roger—which was strange because Roger, a mail order whiz, begged to be part of the team. Later, the team learned he had mortally damaged his previous team, and it had been time to move on.

Meanwhile, the sabotage had begun. Reports that had been carefully proofread went out with embarrassing errors. Schedules that had been carefully synchronized were now way off—people began showing up for meetings on the wrong day, or for meetings that the other party was unaware of. The networking software went down. Even the petty cash account was off, by almost $50.

Everyone was confused. At first it seemed like phenomenally bad luck. But after a crucial file disappeared from the server hard disk, they began pointing fingers. When accused, Roger gave them his best "What? Me?" face, denied everything, and declared he was deeply offended at any suggestion he would undermine the team. And hadn't his schedule been shuffled as well? He was the victim, not the perpetrator.

He was persuasive. It wasn't until a bit of e-mail from one of Roger's previous team members surfaced, asking if the current team members were experiencing any data problems, that Roger was confronted again. No one could understand his motive. It wasn't for promotion, or to make himself look good, or personal vendetta. He was just a crazy, rotten guy. An ogre, who hated his life, his team, his job—everything. An unapologetic wrecker of well-laid plans.

People in human resources consulting will tell you how to handle all kinds of personnel issues. But no one's got much of a handle on what to do with a dark angel like Roger. Dark angels are the beasties in the New Age box, the team poison pill. The brave new world we've been ushering in didn't plan on dark angels being there. But there they are.

There often isn't a lot of incentive to get rid of them. Terminating people is confrontative, unpleasant, and potentially litigious. So we look the other way and hope the madness goes away. A team member with an addict personality may collapse from the weight of his or her own problems. A team member with an ogre personality, driven by some dark rage, may still be a good producer. Team members who go berserk and start hurling large objects about the office telekinetically—well, who are they bothering really?

A team member who is unscrupulous or super-competitive or overzealous is doing exactly what he thinks he was hired to do. Be honest—amoral unscrupulousness is a tried, true pathway to success in many organizations.

Explaining the ten commandments to them won't stop these people. Philosopher and social critic Scott Peck theorizes that evil is not a choice we make but an external force with its own reality, seeking opportunities, viruslike, where it can find them. And it finds them most often in isolated, alienated individuals, who are so estranged by upbringing, circumstance, or by their very nature that no act is beneath them as they roll unstoppably toward their objectives. (Scott Peck, *People of the Lie,* New York: Simon & Schuster, 1983.)

Some people you can counsel, some you can transfer to the company office in Ultima Thule. Some you can quietly let go, and let them paddle off to some new ship to wreck—you may even write the delicately phrased letter of recommendation ("I cannot recommend Kennedy too highly.").

But some people, like the alien being hiding in your hold, leave you only one option. A stake through the heart, before they put one through you.

chapter 12

Leadership Failure

Leadership is the tiredest word in organizational literature. It bears the burden for so much of every organization's hopes. Everyone agrees that "leadership" is vital to teams, like chlorophyll catalyzing the making of sugar. But what is it, exactly, and how does a team without it, get it?

Perhaps the best way to understand team leadership is to notice what happens when leadership isn't there. It isn't pretty.

Things *don't* happen. With no guidance, team members resort to a machine approach to getting work out the door. "When in doubt, automate." Pile up product!

People are upset, disillusioned, hostile to their own enterprise. When work does get done it has a predictable character: mediocre. There is genuine despair among the team because there is no rallying point, no one to vent at, no one to intercede when things go awry, no one to get everyone back on track.

Eventually team members either explode in anger or implode in despair. Or worst of all, they decay in a lifeless orbit. Commitment and energy drain away. Slowly, individuals begin to drift away from the team. By the time the team figures out it is dead, it is really dead. But it started dying the moment its leadership came into question.

If that sounds like almost everything bad that can happen to a team, you're right. Leadership is that important. This chapter is going to look at what makes a good team leader and how the team can help its leader lead, and suggest some new ways of leading that you may not have thought of. Indeed, if leadership is vigorous and intact, few other problems are insurmountable. But from a practical standpoint, few organizations have figured out:

▶ what team leadership is exactly;

▶ how to foster it; and

▶ where it ends and autonomous teamwork begins.

Too often we define or describe leadership the way we see it. Leadership in a teaming atmosphere can look like just about anything. It can look like a good old-fashioned, hierarchical, top-down, leader-led team. The leader is the boss, everyone else does what the boss says.

Or, on the opposite end of the spectrum, it can occur on ultra-flattened, inside-out, molecular, so-called *leaderless teams*. (We prefer the phrase *shared leadership*.) No individual is set above any other, but everyone pitches in to keep the team focused and on track.

No single model of leadership is absolutely wrong, and none is absolutely right. A democratic approach is great for achieving buy-in to team decisions. It creates fewer hurt feelings, less resentment, and better morale. But in crises, or for quick fixes to stop the bleeding or hose down a fire, an autocratic leadership style is just what the tyrant ordered. In time of war, the military model makes terrific sense.

At either end of the spectrum, however, we see good and poor leaders.

A Taxonomy of Lousy Leaders . . .

Here are the 19 most common unflattering epithets for leaders, gathered from our years of experience watching rotten leaders wreck their teams:

1. *The Moron.* Not so much low IQ as a stunted in-the-box, by-the-book approach to thinking.

2. *The Ignoramus.* Next of kin to the Moron; a stubborn refusal to admit new information; closed-mindedness.

3. *The Hypocrite.* A leader who says, "Do as I say, not as I do."

4. *The Daredevil.* The beaver that is too eager, attempting everything and achieving nothing; hoping hyperactivity compensates for lack of reflection.

5. *The Peacenik.* A leader who cannot permit conflict, including the healthy storming necessary to create a strong team.

6. *The Jingo.* A leader who doesn't value diversity and wants to keep the team "pure."

7. *The Spaceman.* So smart no one can fathom what he or she is saying.

8. *The Softie.* The team needs to be pushed, but this leader is too humane to do the pushing. Sometimes you have to be strict.

9. *The Misfit.* A leader with the wrong style or approach for the team at hand. You can have superior skills and talents and still be a Misfit.

10. *The Self-Server.* The worst kind of toxic leader puts him or herself above the team.

11. *The Hermit.* A leader who doesn't really know the team, who can't overcome his or her natural reserve.

12. *The Vacillator*. Inconsistency and leadership don't mix. Set a course and stick to it, at least until the shift is over.

13. *The Hero*. A leader who cannot take a back seat, who has to be in "follow-me" mode at all times. Heroes wear their teams out.

14. *The Nepotist*. A leader who plays favorites, and consigns others to the woodshed.

15. *The Blamer*. A team leader more interested in tabbing a fall guy than in learning from mistakes.

16. *The Alien*. A leader who is oblivious to team members' personal and career needs.

17. *The Coward*. A leader who is unwilling to fight for the team.

18. *The Cinder*. Passive, burnt-out leadership that can no longer generate sparks for the team.

19. *The Traitor*. Leaders must not ever deceive the team, or sell it out. There is no recovery—ever—for betrayal.

What Effective Team Leaders Look Like

Here's one type of leader:

Ted Hoinka is a front-line team leader for baggage handlers at a major U.S. airline. His assigned turf is the plane servicing ramps at Denver's international airport. At least, it's supposed to be. Just as often, one finds Ted at the airline's executive offices, or elsewhere in the system, helping to remedy everything from employee motivation and training issues to knotty baggage and service problems.

But he's the real thing—technically competent and highly effective as a leader. Ted's greatest value, according to his manager, is that he is always looking for ways to improve baggage handling performance—even flying to other stations from time to time to work on interunit problems.

He is a poster child for total quality, for process improvement, and for team leadership, always thinking, always talking things up, always encouraging team members, seemingly always on.

When you first meet Ted you are almost put off by his energy and interest. But he won't let you be put off for very long. His energy is infectious. He gets you involved, one way or another, either directly by collaring you and hitting you up for ideas or resources, or indirectly, as a model. Ted's motto is "Lead, follow, or step aside . . . there are things to be done."

Ted once appeared at his boss's office door, excused himself for barging in, then proceeded to outline what he felt were significant reasons for poor baggage handling and supervisory performance. Ted indicated he was willing to help get together a system-wide group of baggage area chiefs like himself and noodle the problems and possible grassroots solutions. So, Ted concluded, did the boss suppose such an effort would enjoy executive support?

The boss nodded dryly. Not even senior management could discourage this guy.

Here's another one.

Jim Swindal is an engineering manager for a major lawn equipment manufacturer. He's a quiet, unassuming kind of guy, sporting your basic trademark rolled-sleeve white shirt and a "pocket protector." He has the habit of repeating things you say to him. You wouldn't ever place him as the motivating power behind an upheaval, a revolution in team thinking at the company. But he is.

Harvey met Jim at a company-sponsored leadership workshop. Among unassuming Minnesotans, it's rare for people in a training session to have questions. But there was Jim, with more hands up than a squid. "Did anyone here volunteer for this program?"

The better Harvey came to understand the company's internal customer service processes, the more Jim's name kept coming up. Jim led a pilot project on complaint responses. Jim formed a problem-solving team to deal with communications delays. Jim got company executives to join midlevel teams, to get their heads in the game and see what teamwork was all about.

In one case, Jim took over a research group whose efforts were behind schedule, over cost, and riddled with quality problems—and transformed their last nine projects into winners.

They weren't laboratory successes, either—"easy wins." They were real-world situations working with very normal people. This isn't always a prescription for collaborative effort; yet many actually reported they were "having fun."

When folks were asked how Jim was able to accomplish these startling results, they said things like: "helped us to focus" . . . "a lot of personal energy" . . . "helped us get, analyze, and share information" . . . "supported our creativity" . . . and "helped us to discover and stay on the most productive path."

What can you say about Ted and Jim? They sound too good to be true. But they *are* good and true. To us, and to the teams they work with, they are inspirational examples of team leadership succeeding, mainly by caring a whole lot. Both of them are dogged in their pursuit of a better way. And they are so genuine, so enthusiastic, that other people just want to climb aboard. To hear their feats, you would think they are suffering from fatigue or burnout. But they are having a ball.

How do they compare to the leadership of your team?

What Team Leaders Do to Get People to Follow

First, they don't head toward any cliffs.

Second, team leaders must also follow, by knowing what people's needs are and helping to meet them. A starving army cannot fight. A frustrated workforce cannot compete.

When our crystal ball clouds over and we forget what leadership is, we set aside abstract considerations and focus on folks like Ted Hoinka and Jim Swindal. They are the distilled essence of what team leading is about.

Having said that, Ted and Jim are not all that unique. They are like many of the team leaders we have encountered in our travels within, without, up, down, and through organizations. We all read the magazine articles heralding the senior executive heroes who lead their organizations to the promised land. For our money, there are thousands more leaders, at the operating (management) and front-line (supervisory) levels, who have made those top managers successful by continually challenging the status quo, and unfailingly pursuing quality and performance improvement.

Their contributions as team leaders add up to much more than a day's work for a day's pay. They are the points of origin for those small, project-by-project performance breakthroughs that hone their organization's competitive edge to razor sharpness.

An alternative name for a good team leader might be "quiet revolutionary." The best are infectious self-starters like Jim and Ted who cannot help but positively influence others around them.

Their efforts reliably produce a bigger bang for the buck, essentially *adding value* to their organizations through distinctive team leadership activity. From this, we propose a working definition of team leadership:

Team leaders add value by leveraging their organizations' assets and outcomes beyond expectations. The result of this value-adding leadership is enhanced performance in four different dimensions:

▶ *self and others*

▶ *awareness and choice*

▶ *focus and integration*

▶ *innovation and action taking*

What does adding value mean in the context of team leadership? Leaders add value by getting more than required or expected out of what they have to work with—existing human and physical resources. Working cooperatively with other people, they appear to successfully guide problem solving, fix things, innovate, and capture opportunity more often and at a faster pace than many of their peers.

Are we saying team leaders are inherently supermen or super-women, freakish examples of inborn leaderly genius? No. Instead, we say today's top team leaders do whatever they need to do to:

1. perform at a very high level of competence and productivity themselves; and

2. elicit solid effort and performance from the people they work with.

Let us underscore that we are talking mostly about everyday operating managers and front-line supervisors down in the trenches. We are not talking about the executive nameplates on mahogany row.

Team Leaders Leverage Themselves (and Others)

The primary resource available to leaders is the people in their midst, including themselves. First, they leverage high levels of performance from themselves. Then, as surely as night follows day, they leverage a similar level of performance from the people they work with.

By utilizing the power of people, team leaders:

▶ *Project energy.* They provide task excitement, motivation, spirit. Depending on their personalities they can be as quiet and unassuming as woodchucks. Or they can be all over the place, raucous, chattering, in your face. Whatever their personalities, the leaders we have known have all been *activists,* catalysts for positive action, never happy on the sidelines.

In particular, they seem to take care to avoid the negative, declining to join in at the periodic bitch sessions enumerating the many reasons "you can't get there from here." Instead they take the road less traveled, opting to encourage others and, with everyone participating, piecing together solutions to the problems of the day.

▶ *Are involved, involving and empowering others.* Without being obtrusive, they "walk around"—nudging, assisting, helping, asking questions. They put out and they bring in; they share information they have and they build others into new work processes and projects. The result of all this busy-ness is a greater sense of involvement all around. Good leaders recognize that involvement is not an abstract theoretical point. It's something that you live and breathe on the job, and it requires continual practice.

Leaders not only involve others; we have often observed them sharing whatever power, influence, and other resources they have with other team members. Here comes the dread word: They *empower* others to get the job done willingly, rapidly, and well. Leaders appear unconcerned about losing control or sharing power, trading these slight risks for the improved motivation and performance flowing from their empowering efforts.

▶ *Assist evolution and change.* They guide, smooth, and help others map out and explore the pathways of opportunity. In today's churning organizational environment, this ability to evolve and change is absolutely key to survival. But it's rough—change invokes our fear of the unknown and threatens our habits and previous momentum. Our natural response to the need to change is *resistance*.

Leaders understand that foot-dragging is part of the change process, a necessary first stage. Instead of bulldozing ahead, riding up and over the bodies and minds of those resisting, good team leaders plan ahead, involving others early on and communicating what's happening and why to all concerned. Perhaps most important, they help others realistically appreciate what's in it for them. When fear of the unknown is the ailment, knowledge and communication are the medicine. The great leader banishes fear and replaces it with hope of success.

▶ *Persuade and persevere.* Good leaders identify obstacles, then take them out, blocking and tackling to create running room for the team. Instead of knocking people on their backsides, however, they clear the path by winning over those who stand in the way.

We can scarcely contain our amazement sometimes as we watch the different approaches good leaders take to advance team goals. Some come straight at you, insisting on your support and any resources you can provide. Others employ more subtle strategies: bargaining, trading, exchanging, showing the obvious benefits, using third-party advocates, etc. As with Ted Hoinka, many have little positional power; they instead find support from those who do. This task requires skill. It also requires the tenacity of a terrier. They identify a valued outcome, grab it like the leg of your trousers, and simply keep shaking. They persevere. And their persistence is of such a quality that people are turned not off but on.

Team Leaders Leverage Awareness and Choice

Organizations succeed when people within those organizations are aware of the problems and opportunities staring them in the face.

That sounds elementary, but in reality, there are zillions of outfits where the philosophy is "ready, shoot, aim"—where workers go through the motions of performing their tasks without framing in their own minds what issues are at stake, or what alternative actions might be taken. Without understanding, people just do what they have always done—often to everyone's later regret. Good team leaders are people of action, but only after they have pushed for reasoned insight, heightened awareness, and thoughtful choice.

By leveraging awareness and choice, team leaders:

▶ *Look beyond the obvious.* Human organizations are not anthills, where instinct is the best bulwark against destruction; we need to think things through. Team leaders value the search for information and the best feasible choice among alternatives. Successful "hipshooters" are rare among team leaders. Team leaders spend time up front, finding out what questions to ask, analyzing situations, and most especially seeking to involve the people who will play a part of any implementation. Often their inquiry is informal, relying on those with the most relevant experience. Many leaders, however, have no reluctance to take the time, expense, and effort of using more sophisticated techniques. They seem to take inordinate pride in doing quality work the first time and avoiding the distressing necessity of "engineering in the field" later.

▶ *Maintain perspective.* Lose the "big picture" on any team, its overarching vision and goals, and you lose everything. Leaders keep our eyes on the prize, and they foster a "systems view" to guide analysis and action. Team leaders gather a lot of initial and ongoing information. This not only helps team members to understand the processes they are engaged in, it also helps avoid myopic tunnel vision and dedication to a single course of action.

▶ *Encourage pyramid learning.* They stress the need to understand a situation and the options available, and assist others to explore and appreciate the possibilities. They not only investigate and take action, they also seem to hook those around them on the need to absorb what is happening and why. This openness to learning explains the best thing about the best leaders: they are not irreplaceable, because they have taught others so well.

Leaders appear sensitive to the impact of recommendations and changes they propose (or undertake) on other parts of the organization. They tend to ask a lot of *what-if* questions up front, seeking to avoid unintended consequences. Their willingness to consider the organization as a "connected system" not only limits the firing of loose cannons, it pays off in fostering cooperation from other leaders who worry less about the chaos generated when the cannon balls hit.

Team Leaders Leverage Focus and Integration

Focus refers to a team's ability to fix its attention on a goal or task, and integration to individual team members' ability to "get with the program."

Consider what happens when neither are leveraged. Too often in our work with organizations we have noticed a pair of sad but distinct phenomena: one we call the "spaghetti toss" and the other goes by the nickname "turf honcho." In the first case, the organization abounds with unfocused activity and project work—much of it never contributing to overall success. It is as if the organization, not knowing any better, is tossing spaghetti at the wall to see what sticks. In the second case, how many times is the wheel reinvented or something dropped through organizational cracks because of someone's need to put boundaries up and manage their "turf?"

In sharp contrast, team leaders maximize their team's focus and integration. Thus they:

▶ *Target energy on success opportunities.* We have all experienced the problem of too much opportunity and not enough direction. Success opportunities don't arrive with little maps telling you where the treasure is buried. You have to figure that out yourself. Each new path forks off in a dozen different directions. Effective leaders assist team members and others in choosing the right paths and setting the right priorities. Together they focus their efforts toward high-promise activities and outcomes.

We have observed team leaders working with others in some highly collaborative ways, across all kinds of organization boundaries, to test alternatives and get a bearing on the most promising courses of action. Once this focus is achieved, it is as if a green light has switched on for the duration of the project. Teams are able to extend the cooperative spirit generated during these cross-unit, cross-function, cross-level analyses into any later implementation process.

▶ *Foster task linkage with others.* Most of us live in functional cages labeled *Marketing, Personnel, Finance, Operations,* etc. Within these cages or silos we toil in even smaller groups on all the tasks necessary to organizational success. From this narrow perspective, we rarely see and comprehend the size and shape of the elephant entrusted to our care.

Effective team leaders break down the cages and expand people's ways of seeing beyond their narrow tasks. They create a common bond with other teams, and a sense of shared fate and opportunity. Team leaders spend a lot of time working across boundaries. They help folks feel "we are in this together," that with the help of other team members and other teams we can get this elephant on its feet and moving in the proper direction.

▶ *Influence cooperative action.* The task of creating linkage isn't enough. Leaders have to go beyond that to engender a true climate for cooperation. Effective leaders turn fences into bridges. This is not an easy task—cooperative action taking requires lots of set-up, and tons of follow-through. Neither of us could begin to count the number of times we have experienced or observed failure in organizations because individuals or units simply could not cooperate.

There are many reasons for this kind of "dis-cooperation." Some people see no great need for cooperation, and they never bother to develop the requisite skills to carry it off. Others fear sharing "credit" with another unit. Many shut out others until the last moment, when it's too late to elicit genuine cooperation. So it goes. Whatever the reason, we have often found team leaders purposely building relationships across organizational boundaries *pre-need* (that phrase comes courtesy of the mortuary profession).

Note: Team leaders actively identify and influence those who have access to resources necessary to the tasks they undertake.

Thus cooperation is planned and designed into every task. *Note also:* Sensible team leaders rarely burn their bridges to others, no matter what the provocation. Future cooperation is too important to throw away in a moment of emotional indulgence.

Team Leaders Leverage Innovation and Performance

You read about business heroes out there, creating incredible advancements, engineering impossible accomplishments. Nice work, if you can do it. Those we would tag as team leaders are more often ordinary folks who generate improvement bit by bit, consuming our poor, much discussed elephant one bite at a time.

To leverage innovation and performance, they:

▶ *Support creativity.* They challenge team members and others to invest their time, talent and resources in the quest. We aren't talking here about innovative product creation, support for much-ballyhooed skunkworks, etc. Rather, what team leaders seem to value highly are creative approaches to perceived problems or some new "twist" that captures an opportunity. Team leaders are more than just tinkerers—always adjusting, trying out, testing, etc. Ted, for example, is absolutely unrelentingly in a quest for small technical or procedural innovations to produce a better baggage handling process, in service to what he sees as "*his* passengers."

▶ *Take initiative.* Team leaders know that there is no advantage like prompt action. Great leaders are great doers, catalysts who can take *what-if* thinking and galvanize it into action. They take reasonable risks and encourage others to do likewise, and to invest their resources to improve the way their organizations work.

Our experience suggests that team leaders quickly size up an improvement opportunity, involve others, come up with a plan, and then simply "get on with it." In the course of our discussions, another interesting facet of their initiative-taking behavior cropped up: "I'd rather ask for forgiveness than permission," was the express comment made by several team leaders when asked to sum up their approach to getting things done. As the Nike commercial suggests, *Just Do It*.

▶ *Eschew the negative.* Good team leaders accentuate the positive. They continually challenge themselves and their team members to maintain a work environment in which people are glad to participate. This often means creating a "service environment" in the workplace—whether the organization delivers a conventional service or not—and setting high standards of quality and service to customers both inside and out of the organization.

We were struck by the recent comment of a retail supervisor whom we immediately tagged as a team leader. Discussing motivation she exclaimed: "You know, you can whip the 'slaves' and make them work; but you can't make them serve one another, or the paying customer, that way." Her comment put words to our overall sense that team leaders generally seek to create a positive work environment. This fits with our professional view, that a punitive work setting results in "CYA" (Cover-Your-Anterior) team leadership—the exact opposite of what effective team leaders model.

Our experience suggests that folks who feel punitively treated spend their energies grousing about their troubles, "getting even," pursuing outside interests, etc.—and not looking for ways to improve quality or provide service to their colleagues or customers.

Effective team leaders, in sharp contrast, appear to do three things. First, they model and coach positive interaction with others. Second, they either help to get rid of punitive rules and practices or buffer their people from their effects where possible. And third, if you mutter about "how bad it is" within earshot of them, you'll be gently given the opportunity to help make it better.

▶ *Are never satisfied.* The spirit of team leadership is one of continuous improvement. A good leader can never be convinced that existing structures, processes, and outcomes are as good as they could or should be. Again, this shouldn't come as a big surprise.

What's important to note, however, is *how* leaders go about the process. Incremental change—transforming a team one day at a time, one bit at a time—is still a team leader's best strategy for effecting systematic improvement. In part, this approach is forced on leaders by their positions, often well down in the bowels of the organizational pyramid, with limited positional power or material resources. In part, it seems a strategy of choice.

One team leader confided: "Even the biggest improvements I've been a part of happened one small project at a time. Plus, I always feel a sense of accomplishment when I get to see some results early." We see the clear and obvious second element to their improvement strategy.

Leadership Skill Sets

It may help to think of team leadership as comprising four sets of personal attributes and skills: people, character, action, and thinking. Within these four sets are two leadership factors, motivating and hygiene.

Motivating factors are the personal aspects of leaders, aspects they appear to have been born with, so that when we see them in action, our response is "Wow—I wish I could do that!"

Motivating factors include three people skills and three character attributes:

	PEOPLE	CHARACTER	ACTION	THINKING
Leading Attributes (**motivating factors**)	▶ Versatility ▶ Pyramid learning ▶ Feedback	▶ Charisma ▶ Integrity ▶ Altruism		
Managing Skills (**hygiene factors**)			▶ Decision-making ▶ Initiating activities	▶ Problem-solving ▶ Fostering linkages ▶ Assisting in evolution and change

▶ *Versatility.* In a fast-changing environment, this is the most important motivating factor. By versatility we mean more than a generalized "adaptiveness." Specifically, we think of it as the ability to *provide information in the manner in which others want to receive it,* based primarily on an understanding of their personalities. Not "being all things to all people," but being who we need to be to deal with the people we need to deal with. A versatile team leader changes his or her mode of communication to either provide more facts, history, and other data, or more action plans and outcomes, or more options and future expectations, or more concern for people issues. This is all determined by the way the other person needs to view the information.

▶ *Pyramid learning.* The idea of "pyramiding" comes from medicine, where a drug travels from one cell to the next in a pyramiding fashion, eventually spreading throughout the entire body. Great team leaders will share information that they acquire with others and encourage them to do the same, in order to "pyramid" the learning throughout the team and from team to team.

This increases the intellectual capacity of the entire organization, making it a learning company.

▶ *Feedback.* Effective leaders learn how to provide feedback on a regular basis, looking for ways to assist employees in enhancing their skills. This requires a strong social sense—the willingness to reach out to others, but also great tact and delicacy in knowing the right way to praise and offer correction.

▶ *Charisma.* This is a mysterious aspect, which people either have or don't have. We don't mean the kind of creepy charisma that allows some people to lead others into flaming quicksand. Good charisma is a subtle, often unflashy charm that informs the team nonverbally that the leader is in common cause with them.

▶ *Integrity.* The true measure of a person is his or her ability to live in alignment with principled values. We don't mean rigidity; we do mean solidity. Integrity means you don't just talk the talk, you also walk the talk. It starts inside, privately; but it is inevitably obvious to everyone.

▶ *Altruism.* You have to "mean well." There are lots of better things than meaning well, and meaning well by itself makes a woeful epitaph. But unless you do mean well, no team success is worth achieving.

Hygiene factors are called that because they are really habits of doing and thinking that nearly anyone can master—if they put in the time and energy.

▶ *Decision-making skills.* It's often better for a team leader to make a bad decision than no decision at all. For if you are seen as chronically indecisive, people won't let you lead them. There are obvious problems with just "deciding," machine-gun style. When you make a bad decision, you must take the rap for it. If you either "blamestorm" (look for scapegoats), or ignore the mistake, people won't trust you or follow you. Acknowledge the error, however, take responsibility for it, correct it, and make decisions to go in a different (better) direction, and your term will continue.

▶ *Initiating activities.* Leadership starts things. If you are viewed as being more of a stopper, or a reactor, you will not be looked upon as a leader. The concern here is to maintain a balance between initiating too many activities (creating an activity-vs.-outcome-based organization), and not enough (slow, reactive, and nonresponsive).

▶ *Problem-solving skills.* This is about a little thing called competence. No one wants to follow a nitwit. The ability to quickly diagnose problems and implement solutions is key to maintaining the confidence of the team.

▶ *Fostering linkages.* You may be the duke of your own team fiefdom, but if you don't create permeable walls where information flows freely in and out, you will be viewed as small-time, not as a leader. Great team leaders electrify the atmosphere. They create an exciting environment where information, knowledge, understanding, and expertise naturally spread. They create a collaborative environment within which people feel free to share information across boundaries, and create teams where necessary to get specific outcomes achieved.

▶ *Assisting in evolution and change.* Team leaders enjoy a valuable perk: their position allows them to share their views with others. Great team leaders make hay with this perquisite—they help people understand the reasons for team activities, and they provide a rationale for the direction the team is going. There is real power and responsibility for change here. The leader judiciously addresses the passions that create change: anxiety about the past, and hope for the future.

So what are you supposed to do with all this? Incorporate it into your team leadership kit. Think of leadership as a set of stairs where one must master the hygiene factors before stepping up to the motivating factors. One is built upon the other. Having mastered the hygiene factors, you can be seen as an effective manager. Go on to master the motivating factors, and your team will see you as a leader.

The Wrong Leadership

Leadership is susceptible to the same variations of personality we talked about in Chapter 10.

In addition, an unsolvable problem of team leadership is satisfying different people's needs for different kinds of leadership. Your team members may prefer, by turns, a tyrant, a shepherd, a father (or mother), and a pal.

Leaders will make themselves crazy trying to be all these things. Yet to completely ignore individual needs is bad too.

Fortunately, many teams allow leadership to rotate from person to person. A clever team may be able to pit different members against one another, providing each member with the required degree of motivation, instruction, discipline, or approval.

When your team can do that—meet everyone's leadership needs halfway, without skipping a beat—you have accomplished something.

How does a group become that versatile? By understanding and appreciating how different kinds of personalities interact.

Consider how the four main personality types lead, and how each kind of leader signals what approach is being used. Your challenge is to identify your leading style, and to check to see how it is likely to succeed or fail with different team members.

WHEN DRIVERS LEAD

Contribution

Drivers are the task experts. They are results-oriented types whose motto is "Lead, follow, or get out of the way."

Verbally

They get directly to the task at hand, with little or no small talk.

They tend to do more talking than listening.

They direct and control the pace of conversation.

They are forever hauling people back to task when they wander.

They interrupt, finishing teammates' sentences.

They speak in a forthright, direct manner ("I want ..." or "You need to ...")

They are not afraid to challenge teammates' thoughts and ideas.

They ask *what* questions, the kind that lead directly to results.

Nonverbally

They often have forceful, commanding voices.

They are confident, and they show it.

They also show when they are impatient. (Check that watch!)

They let you know when you're done talking.

They can be opaque and hard to read—their facial expressions don't reveal much.

Their offices are functional, with a clock; you will likely see plaques and awards on display.

WHEN EXPRESSIVES LEAD

Contribution

Expressives are the communication experts. They are the enthusiastic influencers whose motto is, "It's not just whether you win or lose, it's how you look when you play the game."

Verbally

They talk about their thoughts and feelings.

They like to tell stories and share anecdotes.

They use lots of adjectives and vivid descriptive phrases. They prefer metaphor to money.

They digress from the point at hand—they can't help it.

They ask the *why* questions—the rationale, the motivational questions.

They persuade and sell.

Nonverbally

They are fast talkers.

They are animated, and use dramatic gestures and facial expressions.

They exude lots of vocal variety—inflection and volume.

They smile and nod their heads a lot.

They can be stylish and fashionably current in appearance.

They are kinetic, and emit lots of energy.

Their offices may be stylish and maybe a bit flamboyant; or they may be somewhat cluttered and jumbled. And hey, check out the toys and cartoons.

WHEN ANALYTICALS LEAD

Contribution

Analyticals are the informa- tion experts. They deal in facts, data, and details. Their motto is, "The facts speak for themselves."

Verbally

They do little small talk or socializing.

There is little disclosure of feelings or thoughts.

They strictly focus the discussion on the matter at hand.

They don't make many errors with facts or details.

They often have large vocabularies.

They ask all kinds of questions—especially the technical question *how*.

They share data and information—often more than others want..

They don't rush to judg- ment. They decide things rationally and systematically.

They may be annoyed by others who are "less thorough."

Nonverbally

They speak slowly and deliberately.

They share logic methodi- cally.

They show little animation or facial expression.

They don't gesture much, either. *Statuesque* may describe them.

They prefer a formal, conservative appearance.

Their offices are functional, with lots of storage space for information.

WHEN AMIABLES LEAD

Contribution	Verbally	Nonverbally
Amiables are the team formation experts. They are good at recruiting people for causes and maintaining their "franchise" with others over time. Their motto is, "Make new friends and keep the old."	They asks lots of questions, to get others engaged.	Listen for a steady and even speech tempo.
	They particularly ask the *who* questions—putting the team together and building constituency.	Look for relaxed body language.
		They listen actively, nodding and indicating their attention.
	They listen, paraphrase, and reflect the feelings of others.	They are pretty quiet.
	They may not be especially quick to disclose what they themselves want.	They dress casually and affect a conforming but comfortable appearance.
	They *love* to engage in small talk.	Their offices are likely to have family pictures, personal mementos, and plants.

Can You "Fix" Poor Leadership?

It is much easier to fix your own leadership deficiencies than it is to fix someone else's. To fix your own, you must simply acknowledge what you will never be good at, and get someone else to take over those leadership dimensions—to share leadership with you. Or you can work to build up and strengthen the weak areas, while drawing upon the team for understanding and assistance.

To get someone else to change is a taller order. People providing poor leadership generally know—sometimes vaguely—they are part of the problem. But in their minds they are convinced they are doing their best, or just behaving the way their personalities allow them to behave. Sure, they could read some book about ultra leadership. But to change, really change? That requires:

▶ courage on the intervener's part;

▶ honesty on the flawed leader's part; and

▶ good intentions on the part of everyone.

Throughout this chapter we have highlighted team leaders involving others, early and often. In so doing, they leverage their own efforts while focusing the skills and cooperative action necessary to tackle "cross-boundary" problems and opportunities.

If your team is having difficulties, the odds of leadership being at the root of the difficulties is very high. You, too, must find a path between the old and the new, to find what works for your group. "What works" is the very heart and soul of good team leadership. Keep trying things, like Edison and his incandescent bulb, until something lights up.

chapter 13

Faulty Vision

've got good news and bad. The bad news is that we're lost. The good news is that we're making great time.

The point of this old saw is that team talent, efficiency, intelligence, and clout are pretty useless unless the team has some clue where it is going and how it is to contribute to the organization's overall strategies for success.

We're talking about vision here, one of the most misunderstood and misapplied ideas making the rounds now. Vision is not a "vision statement." It is not something created in hindsight, or with an eye toward external consumption. It is not something you pay consultants $450 an hour to create for you at a weekend retreat by a warm fireplace and cash bar. It is not printed in bronze ink on a report to shareholders or in a guarantee to customers. It is not really words at all. It is a burning thought, and it exists solely in the heads (and hearts) of the team.

The vision is the thing the team exists to do, defined in ambitious form. It is the thing that leadership makes happen. Without team vision, there is no point to a team.

Vision begins at the corporate level, setting the course for the enterprise as a whole. With the help of leadership it trickles down, uniting the subunits of the enterprise, helping them figure out their role in the bigger picture.

The commonest vision problem teams have is one that is fundamentally beyond their control: the team has a vision, but the enterprise doesn't. It is a sad thing, but no amount of ambition, intelligence, and hard work at the trench level can succeed if the vision of the organization as a whole is a drag. "Returning the greatest possible return on investment to our shareholders," is the best-known offender.

Getting the Picture

Vision is the offspring of hunger. Companies that have succeeded in the past and that had a vision in the past may think the old vision is still in effect. But in many cases it is gone, rubbed clean by the passage of time, complacency in high places, and the high-gloss buffing of corporate communications types.

It is not until a company hits hard times, some rude awakening in the marketplace, that it learns it must have a clue why it is in business. This is a perilous moment. Companies in peril, sensing that they need to stand for something, have a tendency to try to stand for a lot of different things in rapid succession. The resulting wheel-spinning, drum-beating, and horn-blowing can be devastating to that organization's teams. They are like fish in a blender, doing their best against woeful odds.

Having a clearly communicated vision, on the other hand, allows employees and team members to measure their values and behaviors against a company standard. If there is a value clash, people are free to either modify their values or leave. Teams may be better off if some people leave—not that they are deadwood, but because their resistance to the vision of the team had to have a drag on productivity and morale.

Pitfalls of Communicating the Vision

It is the role of corporate leadership to excite senior management about the corporate vision. It is the role of the team leader or leaders to keep the vision alive at the team level. This is a slippery task.

It requires communication, but it requires more than that. It requires exhortation—a little (a little exhortation goes a long way). It requires a kind of nagging—badgering people with the vision a dozen times a day, keeping it in their faces, whatever is necessary to keep that idea obvious and up front for everyone.

More than these things, it requires magic—taking an idea that is in your head and subtly and artfully remaking it in every head on the team. Like the sower and the seed, the leader plants and nourishes the idea, keeps it alive, and allows team members to understand, each one in his or her own way, why it is advantageous and achievable. Team leaders can easily fail in this magical task. Here are some of the standard pitfalls:

▶ *Assigning.* Too often, leaders seek to "assign" the vision. This is what it is, they say. Here are descriptions. Memorize and replicate! It's not a bad way to spread the word, provided everyone on the team is a clone of the leader.

▶ *Dullness.* Leaders whose pilot lights have blown out are not likely to light many fires under team members. Vision is a "must"—emotion is a natural part of creating and communicating it. This is not something leaders can turn on or off, like hydraulic fluid. It must be genuine.

▶ *Waffling.* Leaders cannot experiment, explaining the idea one way to one subgroup and another way to another subgroup. Leaders cannot learn the vision as they preach it. If it is some sort of squirming, evolving target, everyone will miss it.

▶ *Selling.* Another failure is when the leader, often charged up by some consultant or author, tries to replicate the process with himself or herself playing the role of consultant, essentially "selling" the idea to others. It's a bad role, because it positions the leader as outsider. Better to use the natural leverage of a trusted insider, and to hold off on the soft soap.

▶ *Nonaligning.* The proper way to spread a vision is to work with people as individuals to bring their wants and needs into alignment with the team vision. Treat everyone equally. No arm-twisting, wheedling, or cajolery. Show people the respect they deserve as adults and as members of your team, and they will treat your idea with the same respect. You cannot own it for them; they must come to own the idea . . . on their own.

chapter 14

Toxic Teaming Atmosphere

Y ou can't grow gardenias in ammonia, and you can't grow healthy teams in carbon monoxide.

Teams don't thrive in an environment hostile to teamwork. This part of the book discusses ways team environments can go awry, and how to make the air breathable again.

The most egregious toxins in team atmosphere are:

▶ too much competition;

▶ the surprising corollary, too much collaboration;

▶ team tyranny; and

▶ mob behavior.

All of these dangerous gases swirl around every team at one time or another.

So here are guidelines for remixing the team atmosphere to find the right blend for performance. We'll talk about team tyranny and mob behavior first and save the discussion of competition and collaboration for the next chapter.

Team Tyranny

One of the worst and most expensive decisions organizations make is to establish a team system, when all they are really after is an atmosphere of greater collaboration.

Collaboration is a misunderstood commodity. There are managers out there who still associate it mentally with Nazi collaborators—people who cooperated with the bad guys in World War II. So they are against it. Other folks blanch at the mention of collaboration because it sounds tutti-frutti and unmasculine. "What do you mean, share?"

Sigh.

Among people with plural brain cells, however, collaboration is a powerful component of the high-performing mindset. The whole idea of organizations is rooted in the notion of people working together—collaborating—toward a common goal.

Teams do not absolutely require a collaborative atmosphere. There are successful teams operating in overwhelmingly competitive environments.

But leaders of these teams should consider boosting the amount of collaboration in the air. While teams can function in a primarily competitive atmosphere, they will do better when they are encouraged to share information and experiences—including failures, something forbidden in most competitive regimes.

Now we come to an important point. While teams can get by without collaboration, organizations can enjoy widespread collaborative efforts *without teams*. There are ways to get the collaborative spirit short of adopting the teams structure.

What companies should consider, before resorting to teams, is whether they can alter their culture directly, making it a better place to share and think together.

To throw the team switch when all that is needed is an infusion of collaborative spirit is to invoke the dread specter of team tyranny.

Team tyranny is the heavy hand of the organization at large, forcing everyone to do everything on a team basis. The logic is underwhelming: "Teams are great, so let's insist everything be done that way."

As an example, let's pick on one of our favorite companies, Honeywell, now a division of Allied Signal. On the plus side, Honeywell has a long tradition of idea leadership. On the minus side, this appetite for new ideas has occasionally meant getting carried away with organizational fads. A new word gains currency (*quality, reengineering,* etc.) and people lose their minds.

In the late 1970s and early 1980s, when quality circles were just catching on in American corporations, Honeywell plunged deeper into the idea than most. Honeywell's Corporate Human Resources people began modestly, with six well-trained circles. Soon, every executive and manager wanted circles to call their own, and they formed them, without coordinating or training them in any noticeable way. Within six months, the company had 625 down-and-dirty quality circles.

Now, we know what happened to quality circles nationwide—they failed, because they had no power and no one listened to them. At Honeywell, the chaos, confusion, disenchantment, and anger were enormous. Within 18 months, 620 of these teams died miserable deaths, with QC residue left on everyone's hands.

Given that experience, it is no wonder companies like Honeywell are fighting uphill battles implementing total quality management and other team-oriented programs today. All they have to do is look at their hands and remember: *Quality* did this to us.

Well, it's still happening. The only thing that has changed is the word. This time it's *teaming.* Be on a team or lose steam. What sort of person could object to such a good idea as teaming?

Well, any kind of person could, if it makes no sense. Most people, when asked, would say teamwork is good and they probably are on a team or two. The problems arise when teamwork is made mandatory and people feel pressured to form teams for everything.

Team tyranny ("You *must* be democratic, you *must* be open, you *must* share!") sounds ironic and unlikely. But it happens all the time. If you see it happening, make it stop.

Creating a Teaming Environment

Organizations seeking the collaborative spirit of teams without the structural upheavals should consider attacking their existing non-collaborative culture hammer and tongs.

The way to create a collaborative atmosphere or "teaming environment" is neither mysterious nor expensive. You begin by sending a simple but unmistakable signal through the organization: You stop rewarding destructive, competitive, one-up behaviors, and you start rewarding group-minded behaviors.

Then you examine, as honestly as possible, exactly how your organization actually works. Examine behavior, not executive memos. Do people hoard information, keep it from one another? Do they allow one another to fail, without stepping in to provide assistance or encouragement? Is it an organization in which not just functions are enclosed silos, shut off from others by expertise, but one in which every person is an enclosed silo, shut off from others by fear?

If so, you could benefit from a dose of collaboration. Or failing that, napalm.

Take a little thing like e-mail. In a highly competitive environment, e-mail tends to be infrequent, disclosure of negatives tends to be rare, crucial information is typically withheld, and interested parties are conspicuously excluded.

In an environment striving to become more collaborative, e-mail is a common way for people to share news of their progress, or lack of progress. If someone is having a problem or is unable to get over the hump on a project, he or she calls attention to it, and others rally to his or her side with suggestions. E-mail provides a wonderful little collaborative tool—and the cc list, a quick way to include others in the message. Everyone who is affected by your work should be cc'd with relevant messages.

Obviously, you can go overboard with the cc command. You can bring an organization to its knees by including everyone in it in every message. But you get the idea.

Another way to collaborate is through joint staff meetings. Get people outside your function, but whose work yours affects, involved in your planning and reporting.

A third way is to create leadership "bridge teams." If your organization doesn't have formal teams, the leaders of work groups can still get together to touch base and alert one another to upcoming problems, and put an end to inevitable turf wars before they flare out of control.

A fourth way is to fiddle with reporting relationships. Just because you work in a silo does not mean you always have to report within that silo. IT and finance types benefit immeasurably by having direct-line relationships outside IT and finance, with the production or sales or engineering departments, for example. It's like a fresh breath of air—in fact, a blast of real life.

In the broadest sense of teams, it is not possible to have an organization without them. Every time two people talk with a common goal in mind, a team springs into existence, however briefly,

But it is perfectly possible to have a healthy organization without teams in the narrower, structured, "self-directed" sense. Instead of teams, you foster a teaming environment. Which is just as good, and lots easier to manage.

Teams vs. Mobs

In the rush to bestow the manifold blessings of teams upon our organizations, lots of groups get called teams that probably should not be. The resulting groups are too big, too lumpy, quite mismatched, and more than a little confused.

We call these assemblages *mobs*. There are ways to differentiate real teams from fake teams or mobs:

Teams	Mobs
Members recognize their interdependence and understand that both personal and team goals are best accomplished with mutual support. Time is not wasted struggling over "turf" or attempting personal gain at the expense of others.	Members think they are grouped together for administrative purposes only. Individuals work independently, sometimes at cross purposes with others.
Members feel a sense of ownership for their jobs and unit because they are committed to goals they helped establish.	Members tend to focus on themselves because they are not sufficiently involved in planning the unit's objectives. They approach their jobs simply as hired hands.
Members contribute to the organization's success by applying their unique talent and knowledge to team objectives.	Members are told what to do rather than being asked what the best approach would be. Suggestions are not encouraged.
Members work in a climate of trust and are encouraged to openly express ideas, opinions, disagreements, and feelings. Questions are welcomed.	Members distrust the motives of colleagues because they do not understand the role of other members. Expressions of opinion or disagreement are considered divisive or nonsupportive.
Members practice open and honest communication. They make an effort to understand each other's points of view.	Members are so cautious about what they say that real understanding is not possible. Game playing may occur and communication traps may be set to catch the unwary.
Members are encouraged to develop skills and apply what they learn on the job. They receive the support of the team.	Members may receive good training but are limited in applying it to the job by the supervisor or other group members.
Members recognize conflict as a normal aspect of human interaction, but they view such situations as an opportunity for new ideas and creativity. They work to confront and resolve conflict quickly and constructively.	Members find themselves in conflict situations without knowing how to resolve them. They do not differentiate confrontation and conflict. Their supervisor or "team leader" may put off intervention until serious damage is done.
Members participate in decisions affecting the team, but understand that their leader must make a final ruling whenever the team cannot decide, or an emergency exists. Positive results, not conformity, is the goal.	Members may or may not participate in decisions affecting the team. Conformity often appears more important than positive results.

So how do you keep from creating mobs instead of teams?

First of all, sort team membership into two categories: *core team* members and *resource team* members. Core team members are on a project from start to finish with close to 100 percent of their time and priorities dedicated to the project's outcomes.

Resource team members, by contrast, are members of project teams on an as-needed basis. They are just as valuable as core team members, but are only involved with the team as their expertise and input are required.

A resource team member is more likely, therefore, to be on several project teams at any one time. Resource team members may sometimes be asked to participate from the beginning of a project to minimize their learning curve once they become more active in the team's discussions.

Wise teams use these resource team members, who are always just a phone call away, not just as "seagulls" who swoop in as needed to drop their load and take off again, but as valued team members who, over the life of a project, can contribute much more than just an allotment of expertise.

When to Team

If you are *absolutely sure* that a team is what you need, then you must map the team out. This means deciding who the right core and resource team members are, actually forming the team, and following the pathway outlined in Chapter 29 (Moving Teams through Stages toward Success).

Even at this stage it's still not too late to give up on the team approach. You don't need teams when:

▶ decisions are best made by one person

▶ decisions are predetermined

▶ the outcome is not critical to company, division, or department success (like what color toilet paper to buy)

- time is of the essence (a decision by tomorrow)

- the project is either "back-burner" or a low priority

Teams are best used when they are formed to address short-term, high-priority, perhaps cross-functional, single-focused, action-oriented outcomes. You need teams when:

- the wider the input the better the output

- the issue is cross-functional or multidirectional in nature

- the outcome/decision has potential high impact for department, division, or company

Don't feel pressured to form a team because it's the thing to do now. If it doesn't feel right, the heck with it. Form teams only when they *make sense,* and the team output will be greater than the sum of the individual members' inputs.

The Team Biosphere

How do you create a great team atmosphere? First ask, whose job is it to do this?

It is *everyone's* responsibility to create the teaming atmosphere, by fulfilling their roles within the team. We use the phrase *organizational karma* to describe this shared responsibility for climate control—karma being the wheel of consequences, with good deeds and bad deeds alike coming back to us continually. We could as easily use an expression from software development: GIGO—"Garbage in, garbage out." Or as they say in the submarines, when you are all breathing the same air, forgo that second helping of beans.

The life of a team is full of negatives and positives. The negatives are differences in perception between team members and differences in behavioral styles. The positives are an understanding of the characteristics differentiating good team members from bad. All team members need to incorporate positive teaming behaviors into their daily worklife.

Characteristics of Effective Team Members

▶ *Professes a commitment to goals.* It is difficult to work enthusiastically toward some outcome if you don't know what that outcome is. The first thing good team members do is clarify what they're after—what their team goals and objectives are. With this clarified, good team members commit themselves to the outcome. Whatever it takes (within ethical boundaries), they are willing to do.

▶ *Displays a genuine interest in other team members.* People don't have to like each other to work together. That's true in the short term. But good team members develop a genuine interest in the well-being of other team members—not as a team survival mechanism, but as a human bond. It may sound like small talk, but it's more caring: "How was your weekend?" "Is your boy still sick?" "Is there anything I can do?"

▶ *Confronts conflict.* Good team members can tell the difference between confrontation and conflict—between directness and having a chip on one's shoulder. The only way to discover and resolve differences within the team is to open up, acknowledge the disagreement, and negotiate a solution. In fact, effective team members intercede when other team members are in conflict, to help resolve the disagreement proactively. Bad or weak team members turn their backs on conflict and either ignore it and hope it will disappear, or let the other team members battle it out, squandering precious team time and goodwill.

▶ *Listens empathically.* Empathic, active listening is important for anyone, whether you're on a team or not. It is particularly important for open communication between effective team members. Empathic listening means being sensitive to not just the content of the message the other person is sending, but to the emotion behind the message. Good listening means more than shutting up and waiting for your turn—it means getting into the other person's head and heart.

▶ *Practices inclusive decision making.* Good team members run their "first-draft" decision by other team members before they pull the trigger. One never knows what additional inputs you may acquire that may make your tentative decision even better. Not only may you get additional information this way, but you have a communication device online that lets people know where your thoughts are headed—thus minimizing surprises later.

▶ *Values individual differences.* Effective team members look at differences as positive. They respect the opinions of others and view other's perspectives as pluses, not minuses. They figure out how to use the natural differences to benefit the team's outcomes and not as excuses to avoid working with each other..

▶ *Contributes ideas freely.* Good team members don't hold back their ideas. When they have an opinion about something, they express it—even if it's just to support someone else's opinion. If you have an idea about the topic being discussed and you keep your mouth shut (very typical for the Midwest, where we are), you're not being an effective team member.

▶ *Provides feedback on team performance.* Good teams develop a method for providing continuous feedback on how the team is working, what's going right, what's going wrong, and what to do about it. Effective team members also solicit feedback from other team members ("How'm I doing?"). No matter what formal performance feedback system their organizations provide, good teams develop methods for more frequent, real-time, relevant feedback on people, processes, team support structures, and outcomes.

▶ *Celebrates accomplishments.* One of the first questions Harvey asks when doing teaming within an organization is, "When was the last time you folks had a party?" If you haven't had a party lately, you haven't had a formal excuse to celebrate. Maybe your goals are long-term ones, it's hard to break off in the middle and celebrate. So—do it anyway. Effective teams find excuses to celebrate, usually related to the accomplishment of some shorter-term outcome. Look for ways to lift the morale through celebration, both personal and professional.

A Nod to the Predatory Organization

A final, friendly caveat. There are organizations for which neither teams nor a team environment will do a bit of good. These are companies whose culture is unalterably predatory, unapologetic about having a son-of-a-bitch, screw-you personality.

There are thousands of organizations, and hundreds of thousands of departments within organizations, that fit this description, and they are happy with it in their own hellish, Dilbertian way.

For such a company to try to coat itself in collaborative spirit, as if it were some sort of cosmetic powder puff, is absurd. People won't believe the company's intentions for a minute. It will simply waste time and money and fritter away whatever scattered microns of credibility such an organization still commands.

In fact, it just makes it more of a son-of-a-bitch organization, because it has added hypocrisy to its repertoire of treachery and abuse.

Hope we didn't make that sound too attractive.

chapter 15

Competitive Hazards

everal years ago, Harvey was working in a small division of a much larger company that had morale problems and couldn't quite figure out what was going wrong. After poking around, he discovered that the general manager of the division gained sadistic pleasure from watching his teams compete and scramble with each other for limited resources and few rewards.

While interviewing team resource folks, Harvey also discovered that resources weren't nearly as scarce as had been broadcast by the GM. This gentleman simply thought "putting the squeeze on" would heighten the level of team competition. He was right. The resulting friction between teams eventually raised the temperature within teams to the point of team meltdown. The resulting toll on division morale was evident to everyone—except you-know-who.

What we say about this may violate your deeply held principles, but hear us out:

There is no such thing as friendly competition.

Competition, the way people usually mean the word, is essentially a win/lose proposition. The competitor who wins gets the gravy today, and the competitor who loses is going to try to get even tomorrow.

Teaming, by definition, looks to competition's opposite—collaboration. Collaboration assumes that all sides can win; not on every point of every agenda, but enough of a win on the important points, so that staying together as a team remains mutually reinforcing and profitable to all.

Why does competition hurt?

Well, it doesn't always hurt. Healthy competition is an important part of the brute survival instinct. There are times when resources are genuinely scarce, when you must beat out someone else to get your share in order to live. In war, the enemy must die for you to live.

The problem is that Social Darwinist managers are awfully quick to equate the workplace with brute survival and war. They pump up the troops with frightening exhortations to devour the next guy, or be devoured by him.

Some leaders line their office spaces with posters and taxidermy of predatory creatures, to encourage team members to see themselves as eagles, cheetahs, and barracudas. Such displays are considered motivational. In reality, all they achieve is convincing teams that they are working for someone too obtuse to try real motivation—informing people of business conditions, and explaining what they need to do to succeed under those conditions.

The problem with unhealthy, over-the-top competition is that it creates such a toxic trust-deficient atmosphere that teams cannot relax and work together.

Competitors are invariably opponents, withholding information from one another. Collaborators, by contrast, are practically family. They share rather than hoard, relying on one another's experience and expertise to support team outcomes and advance individual goals.

Team members collaborate among themselves to succeed, and they continue to collaborate with other teams, linking arms to achieve the outcomes of the enterprise.

Pitting teams against one another ("Team Red," "Team Blue," etc.), with rewards and recognition going to the team that leaves the others behind, is just that—the pits.

Bottom-line thinking alone should tell you that interteam competition is a bad idea. It promotes results exactly opposite to what teams are capable of achieving. Instead of optimizing resources, you waste the efforts and goodwill of the teams coming in second.

A toxic teaming atmosphere is not always of the organization's making. Individuals and groups within the team have plenty of power to shape the teaming climate. As a young journalist, Mike went from a news office whose team leader was confident, open, and comfortable, to a newsroom where the leader had disappeared into a glass booth. The first newsroom was a place of camaraderie, laughter, and genuine affection; the second was a place of insecurity—of striving and jockeying for survival.

Had management been aware that the team was devouring itself day by day, it could conceivably have stepped in and put things right. But, as is so often the case with teams, management doesn't always give a hoot—and the troubled team is left to stew in its own juices.

It's pretty much the difference between heaven and hell—a matter of perspective.

The Hazards of Collaboration

If competition is "bad," then collaboration must always be good, right?

Wrong. Pure collaboration is as problematic as pure competition. Each has its purposes. But each, practiced to the exclusion of the other, leads to collapse.

Unabated competition, like a Panzer division rolling over Poland, creates a spirit of over-the-top, scorched-earth absolutism, legitimizing whatever means result in victory: treachery, deceit, corruption, murder.

Unabated collaboration is also problematic. It is the nemesis of individuality, progress, diversity, and change.

Here are some of its hallmarks:

▶ *Sameness.* Overly collaborative teams adopt rigid standards and impose them on themselves, foreclosing creative deviation.

▶ *Groupthink.* This leads to purges of perceived outsiders, and stultification of the ideas of insiders.

▶ *Blurriness.* Too much democracy leads to mush. When everyone has full and equal input into a process, you can bet that process will lack focus.

▶ *Slowness.* Consensus doesn't "snap to" the way intimidated agreement does. It is a slow ooze, and teams lose momentum waiting for the ooze to arrive.

▶ *Leaderlessness.* When everyone is encouraged to lead, the end result often is that no one does.

▶ *Defenselessness.* When everyone knows everything, because sharing is so important, there is no confidentiality, and there are no firewalls. Some teams become so intimate and sensitive with one another that they can't function among outsiders.

▶ *Interiority.* Teams who work too long together have a way of becoming cross-eyed over time, focusing on subjects of interest exclusively to the group.

▶ *Mercilessness.* "The many are stronger than the one," is the motto of supercollaboration. It is also the motto of fascism.

Grafting Competition with Collaboration

This brings us to our favorite word: *transcompetition*. Think of transcompetition as the grafting of fruit from the two trees of competition and collaboration. Each tree has fruit that's good, and fruit that's not so good. The job of your team is to combine the best of both trees, the best attributes of each approach, for the task currently facing the team.

▶ *The will to greatness vs. the will to commonality.* Teams require both ambition and humility. Ambition drives us to try great things. Humility lets us survive to try again when we screw up. As great as ambition is, the will to commonality may be greater. It seeks to find win/win solutions, common ground even when positions seem cast in stone. Like the will to greatness, the will to commonality is a talent some people are born with, and most people must struggle to attain. On teams it is a pearl of great worth.

▶ *Focus vs. empathy.* This can also be called inwardness versus outwardness—valuable but opposite skills. The Analytical mentality is capable of focusing on the task at hand to the exclusion of nearly everything else. But empathy is the badge of the Amiable mentality. It is forever scanning the horizon for more to understand, from the outside in. Focus is about me. Empathy is about us. Teams require both in powerful measure.

▶ *Persistence vs. insistence.* These are as different as conquistador and natives, the killer instinct and the instinct to survive. Persistence is heroic, the willingness to die for a cause. Insistence is about survival—in order to keep the cause alive. Every team enjoys a star performance, but every team needs pluggers who will show up every day and do the work that needs doing.

▶ *Results vs. process.* A results orientation is an attentiveness to the *what* of the team: Did we meet our goal? But a results orientation all by itself is a form of tyranny: "Give me my results and don't tell me how you do it." A process orientation is attentiveness to the *how* of the team. Each is important and must be balanced against the other.

▶ *Play vs. work.* Play is a team's genius—its ability to generate, innovate, revolutionize from thin air. Work is why we show up when we don't feel so playful. Business gives lip service to work, but its true ethic is play. Transcompetition means abandoning the pain principle for a pleasure principle: work for the fun of it.

▶ *Personalization vs. depersonalization.* Personalization is the talent for communicating in such a way that the person you are talking to feels the message has been custom-tailored to his or her understanding. Personalization is a precious skill on teams. But depersonalization is also very powerful. It is detachment, the ability to see a thing without regard to its effect on you. How liberating it is to take oneself out of decision making. When detachment comes in, out goes paranoia, disrespect, and the blindness that so often accompanies self-interest.

▶ *Loose vs. tight.* Which structure is stronger, one that is elastic but encourages innovation and experimentation; or one that achieves coherence through the imposition of order? This is an issue every team must resolve for itself. Loose relationships like confederacies permit wider latitude for expression; but tighter relationships, unions, and alliances have the power to effectively underwrite security. Let duration be your guide. If you are in imminent danger of destruction, tighten the bonds between yourself and others. If your survival issues are longer-term, let loose the line and encourage free minds to find solutions.

chapter 16

Communication Shortfalls

our company is insisting it wants great teamwork. Everywhere you look, it's team this and team that. Employees get the message loud and clear. But that's the only message they get.

Once they "team," they feel like they have climbed a tall tree, up to the highest branches, and as far as they can see there's nothing. No mail trucks, no telephone lines, no smoke signals. They're literally up in a tree, left to their own devices, blinking.

Even if you create a team with a magic wand, it must be sustained the old-fashioned way, with lots of TLC—Teaching, Learning, and Communication.

Teaching, Learning, and Communication

Team are about knowledge: how to get it, how to improve it, and how to pass it on. In the old days knowledge was a byproduct of doing business; today it is the primary driver. The distinctions between working and learning have never been fuzzier.

Examine again our list of team dysfunctions: mismatched needs, confused goals, cluttered objectives, unresolved roles, bad decision making, uncertain boundaries, bad policies, stupid procedures, personality conflicts, bad leadership, bleary vision, antiteam culture, insufficient feedback and information, ill-conceived reward systems, lack of team trust, and unwillingness to change. Every one of these dysfunctions represents a failure of learning.

Leaders who are paying attention to their leading, and listening to those they are leading, should be learning their way toward better leadership.

Teams that have struggled with ambiguous objectives in the past should have learned the knack for identifying a fuzzy objective in the present, and be able to discuss among themselves how to bring it into sharper focus.

Team members who have gone up in flames doing battle with one another for reasons having to do with one another's personalities should have learned the futility of infighting and intolerance, and developed the skills for better appreciating one another (or at least not going at one another with chainsaws).

If we are not learning from past experience, it is probably because we are not sharing what we have learned with one another. This is the paradox of communication—that so often we all know the right answer to a question, but for a variety of reasons we keep our mouths shut about it.

An influential article about this paradox appeared years ago in *Organizational Dynamics* magazine (Summer 1974, pp. 63–80). It was titled "The Abilene Paradox: The Management of Agreement," by Jerry B. Harvey. He starts by citing an absurd outing his own family went on one very hot day down in Texas. The family has been sitting comfortably at home when the father-in-law said, "Let's get in the car and go to Abilene and have dinner at the cafeteria."

When polled, every family member said that sounded like a good idea. So they piled into the car and drove the 106 miles in 104-degree heat to Abilene. Once in Abilene, the conspiracy of cheerfulness dissipated. Everyone wanted to know whose idea the trip was. "I just went along to be nice," some said. "I went along because you went along."

The drive to Abilene encapsulated an important rule of behavior: that people miscommunicate as much from good intentions as from bad. And that is death to teams. How many times have you happily consented to do something you didn't want to do, in order to be a "team player"? Effective team members will shudder at that kind of behavior passing itself off as teamwork. It is a form of laziness and cowardice, that every team has to stand watch against. It is a sign that the team is too polite to be a team—it hasn't yet "stormed" its way to better understanding.

Communication Horror Stories

How important is good communication? Pick up this morning's paper, and you will find communication snafus on every page. We guess that over half of the debates and disagreements you read about are less about true differences of opinions than about grotesque misconceptions of the other side's intentions.

Here's how miscommunication undermines a team:

Teammates May and Gloria, who sit on a suburban school recruitment panel together, hate each other's guts. May's goal is to get more kids of color into the school system, even if it means busing them in. Gloria is equally determined to see that the school's excellent standards are maintained. At first they had argued their case before the full panel, but their points of view quickly hardened, and communication between the two came to a halt. Without direct communication, they began to demonize one another, thinking the worst of one another's intentions. The animosity was so complete that they stopped cc'ing routine items to one another, and even scheduled illegal meetings on the sly, without the other one present.

To Gloria, May is a Maoist, willing to destroy the system in order to push her agenda. To May, Gloria is a racist, pure and simple.

Both are dead wrong. May does not want minority kids admitted at any cost. And Gloria is acting purely out of appreciation for a successful program. But their relationship has become so toxic that it is regularly compromising the mission of the panel, to the point that the school board rolls its eyes before the panel makes a presentation. Poor communication has destroyed the panel's effectiveness for the remainder of that school year.

This kind of shutdown is the opposite of the Abilene Paradox, but just as common—it is a mutual conspiracy to betray one another. May won't share what she learns with Gloria; and Gloria intentionally alters what she learns with May, to throw her off the track. Team objectives have been replaced by interpersonal war.

Here's a less venal example:

A logistics team at a Naval supply depot in Virginia is honestly confused. The issue is whom to report to. Their written charter names their own team leader, and her supervisor, as the immediate chain of command. Half the team reports to them. But the team is fortunate enough—well, perhaps fortunate isn't the right word—to have an engaging, charismatic, and high-ranking champion in the depot's executive group. This officer is involved in the tactical decision making of the group, and he enjoys the loyalty of the other half of the team. There are no hard feelings between any team members, yet the overwhelming emotion on the team is uncertainty. Who gets what information? What is the basis for sharing: the leader's need to know or the curious champion's desire to know? Who's in charge? This situation has been going on for over 18 months. The confusion of loyalties, however well-intentioned, is tearing the team apart.

Team members around the world are staring at one another right now, with rhetorical question marks poised over everyone's heads. In their thought balloons are these questions: Do I understand what you just said? Did you get what I meant? Are there truly things that "go without saying"?

Lets break communication down into its base elements, then build it up again.

Learning to Listen

Good communication is a series of checks we run, first on ourselves, and then on the other person. Listening is three-quarters of communication. Do not doubt this, because we have a graphic to prove the point:*

TALKING	**LISTENING TO OURSELVES LISTENING**
LISTENING TO OURSELVES TALKING	**LISTENING**

Talking

Picture yourself "communicating." Be honest now—didn't you just picture yourself talking? And talking is important. If only we said what we have to say more clearly, or more slowly, or simply louder—the world would understand better and we would get our way more often.

In our rush to be heard and understood, we focus way too much on ourselves doing the talking. *We* are the critical factor in communication, it is true. But our listening is much more important than our talking, because our listening determines whether we learn anything, and whether actual communication occurs.

Listening

Instead of beginning in the familiar upper-left corner, with us talking, begin in the opposite corner, with us simply listening to the

---

* We learned this "listening" paradigm from educator Sue Miller Hurst.

other party. This should be the easiest part, but it gives many people conniption fits. *You simply listen.* Ain't no better way to say it.

If you are having troubles with listening, listen up. The other squares, with the more mysterious labels, may hold the key.

Listening to Ourselves Talking

Are we going on too long? Are we embellishing? Are we getting in subtle little jabs at people? Are we "winking" in our speech, assuming things for the group that they perhaps should not assume? Are we annoying the hell out of people with our gabby self-importance?

There are many sources of contamination in ordinary speech, and some of the worst crop up in team dialogue, where we are unconsciously working to express:

▶ our importance

▶ our superior knowledge

▶ our political convictions

▶ our prejudices, which we hope others share

▶ our disdain for the thoughts of a perceived adversary

▶ our insecurity about what others think of us

▶ our lack of stature in the group

▶ our unfamiliarity with the topic at hand

▶ our worry that someone is waiting to gun us down

It is as if we have erected a wall around ourselves to prevent us from expressing our most sincere convictions. An encounter group industry exists to help people breach their walls. If you feel that you are consistently undermining your own best efforts, you might consider getting help of this type. There are a billion good books on how to do this, too. You can descend the interior staircase of your soul and get to work dusting the place.

For our purposes, however, we will simply remind you that whatever you have to say needs only to pass the simple test of teamwork: Are you saying something that is germane to the team as a whole—to its objectives, to its overriding vision, to the tasks it has set out for itself? If so, you are on solid ground, even if you are neurotic and still crave approval.

If not, fix your message so that it is direct, relevant, and respectful of others. People will understand. And lo and behold, the respect you have been craving will start to trickle in.

Listening to Ourselves Listening

We are talking about developing in ourselves a deeper skill of listening, an awareness of our awareness. Why is this good? Because it is a state of respect *for* others that generates respect *in* others. And you will be surprised, once you get to this state and become comfortable in it, how much better your thinking eventually becomes.

Here's a series of checks you can run, as you are doing your best to hear what the other person is saying:

▶ *Are you thinking too much?* If you are busy framing a reply while your teammate is expressing him or herself, you aren't being fair. Forget your reply. Do your teammates the justice of paying attention to *their* thoughts.

▶ *Are you leaping to conclusions?* If you are insecure or hasty, you may be mentally finishing off your teammates' thoughts for them. Let them finish, and listen the whole time.

▶ *Don't analyze.* You may think you're doing the team a favor subjecting its thoughts to your rigorous instant analysis. Quit with the analyzing, already. Think of a conversation as a garden, not a shooting gallery. You can analyze later, after you've paid your dues

▶ *Don't be so cock-sure.* We have a tendency to run what we are hearing against our internal database of what we know for sure.

"That won't work. . . . " "Hey, that violates Robbins Second Law. . . . " "Man, is that stupid!" Who knows, maybe your internal database is wrong (just this once), and the speaker is right. Ask yourself, "I wonder what the second right answer is?"

This square probably sounded the most far-fetched to you when you saw it. We think it is the most important of all. It is a check against your own agitation, your own ego needs, your own impulsive reflexes—your worst communication dysfunctions.

Teams hit the rocks not because of differentness, but because of their response to it. Teams whose members are individually so sure of what's what have ROADKILL stamped on their foreheads. ("So this is what you think of me." "I knew I couldn't count on you." "There you go again.")

Teams whose members are less certain are more open, and more curious about what the next person is really thinking and why he or she is acting that way. Focus on curiosity, and the respect implied in that term will follow.

Feedback

A component of good communication is proper feedback. People, especially teams, need to be told what's what. Former New York City Mayor Ed Koch used to go around asking everyone, "How'm I doing?" It was his signature remark. He knew it was obnoxious— begging for affirmation gets old quick. But he was a shrewd fellow. He knew:

▶ the political value of being known for a single funny catch phrase,

▶ the undeniable human appeal of being interested in the opinions of others, and

▶ the performance value of getting useful feedback.

We're going to be looking at feedback primarily with the last reason in mind. But do not underestimate the power of the other two reasons. Feedback—communication, mutual evaluation, keeping score—is powerful stuff. Good, continuous feedback is like gasoline to a team ready to roll. The shrewd team leader keeps it pumping, for all the right reasons.

We live and work in an information-driven society. We measure everything, and we look at key measurements (monthly unemployment figures, Consumer Price Index, our kids' report cards, our spouse's Visa card statements) to see how we're doing and where we stand.

Teams, too, need to know how they're doing. It is a kind of hunger, a voracious appetite to measure what they are doing every which way:

▶ feedback from one another, and

▶ feedback from team leaders;

▶ feedback from "customers," and

▶ feedback from the organization they are part of;

▶ feedback in the form of numbers, and

▶ feedback in the form of words;

▶ feedback that is scheduled, formal, and official, and

▶ feedback that just happens;

▶ feedback on the long-term, big picture, and

▶ feedback on the here-and-now, itty-bitty picture.

Feedback should be continuous, so that every team member has a living thread of information about "How'm I doin'?" that he or she can use to tailor a workstyle that contributes to top team effectiveness.

Surprises

If you give a team member good, honest feedback and he or she is taken aback, something is wrong. Chances are the team waited too long before clueing in the errant team member. That's why continuous feedback beats periodic evaluations—mistakes don't have time to become habits. If you put off corrective feedback too long, the person in question will resent you for it. "Why didn't somebody tell me?" Semiannual evaluations are for the birds. By the time people find out where they are coming up short, it is too late. And it feels like Judgment at Nuremburg.

Soft-Pedaling

The most important feedback we can give is often negative. But it is unpleasant. We daresay it is even more unpleasant to give negative criticism than it is to receive it—and that's saying something. The worst, worst, worst thing you can do is ignore it or minimize it. For want of a nail, the war was lost, as Poor Richard was wont to say. Replace the nail now, before a small problem grows into something humongous.

Good News/Bad News

No one takes criticism well, so we have to give it with great care. This means walking a line between compliments that don't ring true and honest, helpful support. People can tell when you are "dressing up a dressing-down." When you have something good to say, focus on the good. When the news is not so good, be direct about that, too. It's pleasant if you can convincingly shore up an errant team member with a word or two of friendly support. But it is hard to be convincing about such things, and there is the danger of miscommunicating the correction. The best thing is to say what you need to say. In the end it is the most respectful way to handle the problem.

A Concluding Question

We have been discussing feedback as a top-down phenomenon. Team leaders monitor their teams and provide regular feedback and evaluation. Bosses and supervisors from outside the team provide it as well.

Here's the question: Can a self-directed team self-monitor?

Good question. Without all team members having the designated role of feedback-giving, feedback becomes an ad hoc, undocumented, informal process. Not bad, but not great. Somehow a team must find a way to flush true communication into its system. Chances are there is a lot of vague feedback already occurring, and it may be useful:

"By the way, Georgia, I liked the drawings you came up with in the report."

"Rewrite this for me, will you, Dave—you're so much better at that than me."

"Ravi, I'm having problems importing the file format you're using. Can we agree on a different standard?"

Even informal groups can create formal structures. A free-floating team can institute official carping sessions, where they can air out problems they are having with one another. Make it friendly, so the gripes don't overwhelm other kinds of feedback. And make it problem-solving oriented, so people leave feeling positive.

A leaderless team can have a process by which every member has another member to serve as a sounding board, with the idea that they meet once every week or so, over lunch, and discuss problems, worries, and performance questions. The two take turns mentoring one another. There should be a compact that the dyad be more than a back-patting session—maybe the team can draw up a series of hard questions to go over each time, so that the pairing accomplishes something.

And have doughnuts available. People like doughnuts.

chapter 17

Rewards and Recognition

T he happy team books of the past decade suggested that it's such a great thing to be on a team that people will do it for free. Our observations do not bear this out. Work is an investment people make. They demand a return on that investment. If you do not pay them, they will not work. This principle of human resources was established during the late Mesozoic Period, in the case of *Og vs. Magog*.

No, pay/don't-pay is not the issue. The issues are *how* and *whom* you pay. Teams are a new thing, but except for a few departures (paying in stock, profit-sharing, gainsharing), not a lot of quantum thinking has been applied to compensation, rewards, and recognition for teams.

We shall attempt to apply some now.

This Book's Sole Sports Analogy

Consider the following fictional scenario, from the Trans World Stadium in St. Louis.

Quarterback Curt Warner has a bonus in his contract. It says that if he plays 50 quarters through the regular 16-game season, he earns a $2.75 million bonus. Seemed like a good idea when the bonus was drawn up—the team wanted to reward him for staying healthy.

But here it is, the last game of the year. His team, the Rams, are tied for first place with the division rival Atlanta Falcons. Warner is playing. The score is tied 17-17, but he's thrown four interceptions. His defense has been on the field all day. One more turnover and they can kiss the season goodbye. Warner knows his arm is hanging by a scrap of tendon, but he's keeping mum. Coach Mike Martz grabs him on the sidelines and tells him, "I'm taking you out." Warner replies, "Do that and I'll sue you."

Huh? The problem here is that the reward Rams management thought was so clever has come back and bit them on the behind. At a moment when every player should be focused on the team goal of winning the division, the fictional Warner is willing to sink the team to claim his $2.75 million. In his own mind he is only doing what was asked of him. And a system of rewards focusing on individual action is about to undo the entire team.

Something Rotten in the State of Rewards

Despite some talk about team rewards, most team members are paid today exactly as they were paid in the days before teams, on a strict individual basis.

We are rewarding individuals when we should be rewarding teams or the workforce as a whole. Not that there cannot or should not be "stars." Once again the 80/20 rule comes into play: 20 percent of team members accounting for 80 percent of team success. But a successful team is always chipping away at the 80/20 rule—it seeks to get the very best out of all its members.

In the typical Japanese corporation today, about a third of all compensation is based on company performance.

On the other hand, we ask unions to help increase productivity when they know that success means decreasing the workforce, laying people off—the exact opposite of their best interests.

We establish bonuses to motivate people, but the bonuses don't motivate because they are automatic or guaranteed.

We patronize team members by dangling carrots in front of them. My, isn't that an attractive carrot?

We set up policies and procedures to instruct team members to do the right things without being supervised every moment—but we fail to shape a culture within our organizations that lets teams and team members feel secure doing the right things.

Teams will not carry out business objectives if doing so puts them at risk.

Teams don't fail because the people on them are stupid. Nor because they don't enshrine the virtues of customer satisfaction, quality, and the rest. Teams fail when the people on them don't feel safe going after their own stated goals.

The Importance of Security

What does "security" mean? It means a company professing to be serious about quality mustn't punish teams who undertake initiatives to complete their mission.

It means that team members exhorted to use their minds must feel free, and even encouraged, to disagree with one another, and with management as a whole.

It means that teams encouraged to increase productivity will not be "rewarded" for their success with layoff notices. We all claim we want teams to "take risks"—but if the company is in a downsizing free-fall, how much risk are teams likely to take?

The Real Culture

Managers often think they can influence behavior based on quarterly goals or semiannual financial targets. The opposite is truer; it is day-to-day culture—the informal signals about what is valued and what is not—that drives behavior more than anything else. So how do we un-confuse our systems of rewards? By getting back to basics, and creating a system of rewards that reflects reality.

The challenge is to find mechanisms to help us influence team performance that are consistent with the strategic direction and priorities of the organization as a whole.

We have flexibility in altering our rewards system that we aren't even aware of. To tap into this flexibility, we need to ask several questions.

What Rewards Do Teams and Team Members Value?

The issue every team leader faces is how to get the people reporting to you committed to your goals. There is no one-size-fits-all method for achieving this alignment. Industries differ widely from one another, and the kinds of people who choose to work in one industry—a government service bureau, say—are usually different from the kinds of people who choose to work in a sales organization. Different companies have different kinds of rewards, because they want to attract different kinds of people.

People also have different compensation needs at different stages in their career. The needs of a 25-year-old are very different from those of a 50-year-old in the same organization.

What Motivates People?

Most people will chime in and say cash. But it isn't that simple. Cash can be a feeble bond if working conditions are unhealthy or the work itself is unsavory. For skilled workers there must usually be something besides cash on the barrelhead—security, the feeling of being appreciated, being left alone, pleasant working conditions, time off to recoup.

For some people the best reward of all is the work itself—the challenge of an engaging job. For some it is the interaction with other skilled team members. For some it is the intellectual gratification of addressing and solving a knotty problem.

Say It with Cash

Still, for many people, and many occasions, the best reward in a commercial enterprise is good old money. Three financial options that have met with success are *gainsharing, profit sharing,* and *employee ownership.* The idea behind each is to reward teams when they perform well. Each method has the side virtue of giving each team member a shareholder's stake in the organization, and a sense of true participation in the organization's overall strategy. Each also falls short of the stated goal of motivating people to commit to organizational objectives.

▶ *Gainsharing* is a system whereby money or resources that are saved by a team are returned, in some degree, to the team. Gainsharing is in use at many thousands of companies. It links people with organizational success.

Problem: The easiest gainsharing plan to set up is a companywide or locationwide system. It is harder to measure the success of most kinds of individual teams in dollars—design, research, quality improvement, and problem-solving teams being exceptions.

▶ *Profit sharing* is better known and more widespread than gainsharing, perhaps because the idea is simpler. Every year or quarter, a dividend is paid to employees based on corporate- or divisionwide performance. Usually, the money is tumbled in with the worker's retirement or 401(k) plan.

Problem: Profit sharing is individual-oriented, and organizationwide. It doesn't address team performance. Also, deferred rewards like retirement money never quite feel like rewards.

▶ *Employee ownership.* These plans go by such names as stock option plans, stock purchase plans, and employee stock ownership plans.

Problem: Ownership is great, but some companies aren't worth owning, even with terrific workforces. Teams can succeed and stock price may still decline.

Reengineered Rewards

As organizations continue to reengineer and overhaul themselves, cash takes on a new face as a team reward. Tomorrow's team members will likely find that the new workplace provides less, not more, opportunity for promotion. Companies getting rid of unnecessary management levels will not be anxious to promote you to one of those evacuated positions. Thus, team members may find themselves stuck for many years in fairly static positions—by title, anyway. You may spend twenty years, for instance, with the job title "customer service representative."

Sounds terrible, right? But these twenty years will not be at burger flipper wages. In the reengineered organization, companies will need to compensate good team members for their vertical limitations with nice juicy horizontal rewards.

Think about it. A team member with deep experience in meeting customer needs will be a very valuable person, able to command substantial salary and benefits.

Downsizing is a drag, but survivors who deliver the goods to an organization's customers will be richly rewarded: "I'm a customer service representative. And I make $155,000 a year."

Team-Defined Rewards

Management gurus insist that teams should not define their own reward system—that's "putting the monkeys in charge of the chicken coop." But we think it's an approach worth considering anyway. Team members shouldn't set their pay levels, we agree; but they may make valuable contributions to defining benefit choices and designing recognition programs.

You may be a distinguished mind reader, and you may have picked the perfect reward last time. Next time, however, why don't you ask workers what *they* would like as an incentive or reward? You can't predict what will light a fire for them.

Consider team-proposed rewards as a kind of compensation laboratory. Yes, there will be some bad ideas, but there will be some that you would not have thought of in a million years by yourself, and the best will carry over to other teams as well.

Thirteen Low-Cost or No-Cost Rewards

We have so far focused more on compensating business teams than the nonbusiness teams we are all on, such as in volunteer organizations. But nonbusiness teams have been the pioneers in alternative rewards.

How do you let workers know on a team basis that their efforts are appreciated? "Cash is always in good taste," is a well-worn adage. It's also an untrue adage—reward a deed done out of simple decency or honesty with a few bucks and watch the proud smile on the good-deed-doer's face disappear.

Few team leaders have a laundry basket of financial favors to hand out to deserving team members. But there are still lots of no-cost or low-cost ways to keep team members involved and in the mood to perform:

1. *Establish a prize.* Establish a quarterly "most valuable team member" award that teams themselves vote on. Establish a "biggest improvement" and "best team spirit" award, too—it helps keeps individual performance stars from getting all the attention.

2. *Get 'em involved.* People who have an impact on reaching goals appreciate being part of forming those goals. Bring your best people into the planning process and they will walk through fire for you.

3. *Power to the people.* What better way to spur productivity than to give proven achievers authority to spend a few bucks to increase sales, please customers, or improve critical processes? (But use the Empowerment Grid, so the infusion of new power doesn't blow the team up.)

4. *Not rich, but famous.* Establish a "Hall of Fame" in your unit or department—a gallery of pictures, trophies, and plaques, with an emphasis on winning teams as well as winning individuals. If you don't have a physical location, do it in your print materials, or on your Web site.

5. *Praise in print.* If you have access to internal publications—newsletters, magazines, tabloids—get word of your people's performance to the editors. Both the editors and your people will be grateful.

6. *If they had a hammer.* Everyone's dying for a faster laptop, cell phone, or wireless e-mail kit. See that your top producers have access to your best tools.

7. *Meet the boss.* Getting a chance to hobnob with the group VP or even the CEO is a big deal, and shows you care about your people's career tracks.

8. *Share the spotlight.* A pat on the back means more when it occurs in plain view of coworkers. But be careful your reward ceremonies don't divide workers into winners and losers, or over-stress individual achievement.

9. *Privy privvies.* Everyone likes perks. Admission to the executive washroom, dining room, or gym. A parking place close to the building entrance. A direct phone line, bypassing the switchboard.

10. *Free lunch.* Many companies purchase annual tickets to sports events, concerts, and other events, and many take travel, entertainment, and other goods and services as trade-outs. Why not share them with the people who make your unit a success?

11. *Stock options.* If your company isn't up to a companywide stock purchase plan, consider a smaller-scale plan as a reward that binds your winners even closer to the company's fortunes.

12. *Lavish them with attention.* Years ago, the famous Hawthorne experiments showed that people show more interest in their work when management shows interest in them. Paint the office, move things around, invite juggling clowns for lunch—anything to break the monotony and show that you care.

13. *Show 'em you care.* A good team works like a family, and is fueled by respect and even affection. Let performers know their contributions are appreciated by you, personally. Look them in the eye and tell them that. It beats dinner for two at the Pump & Munch, hands down.

Who Decides Who Is Rewarded?

The greater the likelihood that the person you report to controls rewards, the greater the likelihood they will influence your behavior. At bureaucratic organizations, this logical rule of thumb doesn't apply—simply come to work and keep breathing and you get everything that's good. Reward systems cannot be automatic or remote; to be effective they must be managed from close range. Are rewards stipulated by the same entity that measures individual and team performance? They should be.

Should team leaders and team members be part of the individual evaluation process? That's a tough call. People on the team have the best knowledge of the value of one another's work. But team members must not be put in the position of politicking one another for promotions and raises. It's best to have the evaluation occur outside the team, with some evaluative information supplied from within.

What Behaviors Are Rewarded?

Are workers rewarded just for showing up every day? For individual performance? Group performance? Organizational performance? Only a company with a narrow array of functions should be using a single reward approach. It is natural to use incentives to compensate sales people. But if it is good to encourage people in sales, why leave out support functions? The entire bandwidth of a company's workforce must be looked at to find rewards that push people together toward organizational success.

Rewards must be for achievements that matter, not noncontributing, nonvalue-adding activities. People must feel their work is important. People who cannot make the crossing to be more accountable even with training must be winnowed out and replaced.

Most organizations spend an inordinate amount of time trying to use their merit budget appropriately. One of Wm. Edwards Deming's Fourteen Points, however, is that merit raises be abolished. Not only are they destructive of team spirit—each member's raise coming at the expense of every other members' raises—but they just don't work. Splitting 4 percent into x number of shares evenly at the end of the year is not an incentive. By definition, you offer incentives *before* the fact, not after.

This is such a simple idea—aligning your team's reward and performance with its business objectives. All it takes is clear thinking, some careful study, and the honesty to see what your organization is really saying to its teams.

chapter 18

Trust Hell

On November 2, 1999, one of those increasingly frequent events took place—a man with a pistol walked into a building and began firing.

What made this instance relevant to us is that the seven people the man shot and killed were not randomly selected; they were his work team at Xerox Corp. Within ninety seconds Byron Uesugi, an employee at Xerox's technical services division in Honolulu, slaughtered everyone he had been meeting with for the previous 36 months.

Every year about 1,500 people are killed in workplace violence, and about 250,000 nonfatal physical attacks occur. Typically they are not random; attacks are typically peer-on-peer or against supervisors. The attackers are the ultimate dark angels, bringing bloodshed to their team instead of team spirit.

What these attacks illustrate to us is just how bleak teams can become when the fundamental element of trust is no longer there. We don't know what the dynamics of Uesugi's team were, or what his complaint was. But something had to be drastically wrong, a perceived betrayal deeper and darker than a well, for Uesugi to snatch his teammates' lives.

The Blood of Teams

We struggled to come up with a suitable metaphor for the importance of trust. We tried *food*—"Trust is the food that nourishes a team." Good, but not great. We tried *fuel* and *gasoline*—explosive, but still not strong enough. We tried *oxygen,* and we knew we were getting closer.

Then we hit on the perfect metaphor: *blood.* Trust is the blood of teams—the river that carries it along, that pulses with life, that brings thought and power to everything the team attempts.

And a team trying to operate without trust—trust from the larger organization, trust in the larger organization, trust in one another—is like a body thinking it can go about its business after all the blood has been drained from it.

Now that we have a metaphor, we can describe what we hate. Do you know what we hate? We hate the Dilbert comic strip.

Not that it isn't funny—it is funny, savagely so. Mark Twain would doff his hat to Scott Adams' brilliant barbs.

What we hate is that we live and work in an environment so accustomed to betrayal that we pin funny examples of it on our cubicle walls, and celebrate its dark wretchedness.

Although it is healthy on our part to find humor in the bitterness, it is appalling that such bitterness fills every cup. A team without trust is in team hell. No truth is heard there, only cynical laughter when someone new shows signs of caring.

We've been living with teams for the past two decades, and it breaks our hearts that the common coin for every kind of team, after all this time, remains disappointment. Become invisible, go into any organization, and watch people, and the same patterns emerge:

▶ People don't tell one another what they really think, for fear they will face recriminations.

▶ Team leaders pursue incremental, safe courses of action, because it is safer than trying something new.

▶ No one talks about the real problems, because all agree that no one really wants to solve them.

▶ People's work lives are a charade. They go uncritically about pointless behaviors because pointlessness is the status quo, and fear has cemented it in place.

We're going to go on and on in this chapter about how to create an environment of trust, and some of it will sound Boy Scoutish. Against the harsh rigors of the workplace, "trust" seems weak and without substance, like dandelion fluff that blows away with the first puff of air.

And that is the tragic truth about trust. It is extremely fragile.

The Stinking Corpse

In the chapter about team leaders, we described what happens when leaders lose credibility with team members. A single act of betrayal, and an otherwise well-meaning leader is hung out like a stinking corpse—out of the loop, ineffective, unable to perform.

What is true of team leaders is true of all team members. A slender thread binds dissimilar people into a team: the willingness to keep listening to one another. It does not take much in the way of betrayal—a false statement, a misunderstanding not cleared up, evidence of self-serving above team-serving—to snip that thread.

Distrust is really a very rational thing. It can be described as the psychological dynamic of *closure*. When we lack information about someone or something, it is human nature for us to fill in the gap with negative information of our own making.

When I don't know you or your intentions, and your behaviors don't seem quite right to me, I assume the worst. If I don't know that you are telling me the truth, then in my mind you probably aren't. This xenophobic reflex or suspiciousness is a survival mechanism created by human beings to maintain our sanity— and to prolong our existence in the face of what is unknown and frightening.

In a team situation, loss of trust means instant banishment to a realm outside the inner team circle where no one pays you any attention. Worse, when what we are told conflicts with what we see, our belief dies. In the movies and in life, there is nothing more profoundly insulting than calling someone a liar. Being called a liar negates your existence and negates any hope of a relationship. With the death of belief dies confidence, rapport, the team relationship.

Stephen R. Covey, in *The 7 Habits of Highly Effective People: Powerful Lessons in Personal Change* (New York: Fireside, 1990), describes trust as a kind of bank account. In a new relationship, each side begins with an automatic amount deposited—let's say $100. That amount in your account will grow immeasurably if you behave in a consistently reliable and trustworthy way. Or you can fritter away your $100 with minor acts of dishonesty and betrayal, and before you know it, your promises and explanations come back marked NSF.

Restoring trust once you allow the account to deplete itself is a tall order. Like the boy who cried wolf, you have no basis upon which to rebuild trust, and you will be penalized—although it will seem unfair to you—for a long time, no matter how honest your intentions.

Several movies (*A Clockwork Orange* comes quickly to mind) have been made showing how a reformed individual will continue to be disbelieved and even abused after he has "gone straight." A single act of trustworthiness does not outweigh a single act of untrustworthiness—not by a long shot. You can't undo the harm of betrayal with a single act of heroism or generosity that will make everything else you said or did go away.

Nine Strategies for Creating Trust

The very best way to repair a broken bond of trust is to not let it be broken in the first place. If that is no longer an option, you have a long road ahead of you, winning people back to your confidence. The only way we know is to keep slogging. Tell the truth. Keep your promises. Be reliable. Rebuild your account using regular, small deposits. It may take years of faithful, timely payments.

When you can't be perfect on any of these scores—and who can?—acknowledge it. Explain it. Ask for forgiveness. And promise to work to keep it from ever happening again.

As a prerequisite for building trust, team leaders and team members must:

1. Have Clear, Consistent Goals

We said way back in Chapter 5 (Misplaced Goals, Confused Objectives), that a clear, acknowledged sense of where the team is going is essential not only in giving a clear sense of direction, but as a foundation for trust: If you don't know where you're going, that's probably exactly where you'll end up.

If I don't know what we're supposed to be doing and where we're heading as a team, my tendency is to be guarded and defensive, for my own self-interest and survival. I will find it difficult to buy in to the team purpose and commit to other team members when I feel left adrift and uncertain. As a result, my trust level will be low.

Having goals that are both clearly stated and consistently supported helps me establish a foundation of trust that will strengthen over time as the team moves in a predictable direction toward agreed-upon outcomes.

Many teams are plagued by a series of ever-changing priorities and direction that leave team members bewildered and disillusioned. Many team members will find this inconsistency intolerable—and they will resort in their frustration to self-indulgent, team-indifferent behaviors.

When this happens, it is important to step up communication drastically, to reassert the purpose of the team. Think of communication and trust as being yoked together. They rise together, they fall together. The less the communication during times of change, the lower the trust and commitment level of team members.

2. Be Open, Fair, and Willing to Listen

For many centuries, the Chinese had stringent guidelines regarding who got into heaven and who didn't. First, the gates to heaven were only open to Chinese leaders and royalty (peasants spent eternity in rice paddies). Before leaders could enter, they had to obtain a "mandate to heaven"—sort of like a Get Out of Jail card. One of the key requirements for obtaining this mandate was to be open, fair, and willing to listen to their people. This explains why, even today, senior Communist geezers nearing death have a tendency to loosen the reins of tyranny a bit (a wee bit—they are only hedging their bets, after all).

The same principle applies today in terms of building a sense of trust:

The more open, fair, and willing to listen individuals are, the more they are likely to receive the trust of others (both on and off their team).

"Fairness" must be built into the conversation. People need to hear the word "fair" come out of your mouth: "I'd like the outcome to be fair to everyone." Or, "It's important to me that people feel the process is fair."

Show a genuine interest in what the other person is saying by learning and practicing active empathic listening skills. Set up ways of making yourself accessible to others—an open door policy. These are all ways of starting the trust-building process.

The injunction to be open, fair, and willing to listen is obviously valid for team leaders, but it is equally legitimate for team members. On a team of true collaborators, there can be no outsiders, secret-keepers, or (apparent) conspirators.

Being open means, in large part, letting go. The history of management is the chronicle of a few individuals exercising control over the rest. It does not take a Ph.D. in psychology to see that there is an inverse relationship between control and credibility. Those with the tightest grip on the information at their disposal are the least trusted—again, the mind paints in what it does not know with negative assumptions.

To have credibility, you must relax your grip of control over others.

3. Be Decisive—and How

Nothing sucks the air out of a team faster than having outcomes that need to be achieved when no one is making any decisions to draw nearer to those outcomes. Particularly the person or persons "supposed" to be making those decisions.

Are you a fan of frightening truisms? Try this on for size:

When it comes to building trust, even a bad decision is better than no decision

People just don't trust people who are indecisive (see the explanation of "closure" on page 169). Sometimes, trust dissolves not because decisions are being neglected, but because the team objects to the way the decision was made.

Let's say a team arrives at a decision point in a project. One team member expects consensus. Another expects the boss to decide. A third expects some sort of subcommittee recommendation. What is this team in? Deep weeds. Team members' expectations are thwarted. They become frustrated. Then angry. Motives come into question. Trust is last seen taking the expressway out of town.

This may seem overly cautious but it is not:

Before teams can make important decisions, they must decide how to make those decisions.

4. Support All Other Team Members

Loyalty is a linchpin of building team trust. The concept comes from family life. If you've come from a large family (say, three or more siblings), you know everything there is to know about sibling rivalry. You occasionally beat up on your brothers or sisters. You also, we are sure, protected these same siblings from others who wanted to beat them up. That (the latter, not the former) is what support is all about.

A team is a family.

Fights will occur, but you keep them inside the team. You don't broadcast your dirty laundry to others. You protect team members from becoming victims of nonteam-member abuse. Given the opportunity to agree with someone else about a team member's errant ways, you stick up for that member instead. (Think about it: how much would that person trust you if you badmouthed your fellow teammates behind their backs? Not very.)

5. Take Responsibility for Team Actions

This is a hard one for some team members to get. If something goes wrong, you don't point fingers; you take personal responsibility for the actions of the team as a whole. This is true whether you are team leader or not.

We know of one organization whose teams had a crest which represented their lack of trust. It was arms crossed in front of their chest with fingers pointing in opposite directions.

Finger pointing destroys the very fiber of teamwork.

Blaming convolutes the team process. Who will speak freely, offer ideas freely, and provide honest critiques knowing someone on the team is going to come down on them with a sledgehammer?

It is much better from a trust standpoint for someone to see you as a "stand up and be counted" type of person, not blaming others on the team for failures. Not, "our team doesn't make mistakes," but "our mistakes are team mistakes, and we learn from them and move on."

6. Give Credit to Team Members

Albert Einstein offered this choice piece of wisdom:

"Nothing is yours until you give it away."

This means if it's acknowledgment you want, be generous with what you have done.

Maybe the germ of an idea was yours, but didn't it require the whole team to nurture and expand and apply the idea to the task at hand? The prima donna who insists on mopping up all team applause is probably a very valuable member—but in his very talent lies the seed of team destruction.

Shine a light on others on your team. But shine it sincerely. If it's done in a superficial or artificial or unctuous way (think: Oscar thank-you speeches) you'll kill, not cultivate, trust. But if done with genuine recognition for teammate accomplishments, trust will grow.

Can you be sincere? Can you share? Most of us are pretty selfish and self-protecting, so giving credit to others does not come naturally. It's something to work on.

While you're working on it, be very clear on something: one of the worst things you can do is horn in on another team member's glory. There is nothing more aggravating than to have someone else (like the team leader) take credit for your (or another's) work. (Think: political campaign speeches.) A team member who steals another team member's thunder—what can you say?

Smart guy, Einstein.

7. Be Sensitive to the Needs of Team Members

Work is hard. It can be tiring, frustrating, often painful. So we appreciate it when teammates indicate that they understand the pressures, and sympathize. We're not talking about pity, or playing the tragic violin, or treating one another like children. We are talking about fellow feeling—giving one another the occasional human sign that we understand and appreciate.

The best way to build up a strong trust bank account is by showing awareness of and sensitivity to the needs of other team members.

Showing fellow workers that you are genuinely concerned about their struggles—at work or home—allows them to feel comfortable with you, and increases the likelihood of reciprocal understanding.

On a less intimate level, it means being sensitive to people's practical preferences. For example, there is a best way to communicate with every person: face to face, in writing, e-mail, voicemail, with a lot of details or not, with recommendations or not, etc.

Let the other person know you are trying to relate to them within their comfort zone, not yours. It takes flexibility and thought on your part—but with a handsome payoff in their willingness to hear and act on your thoughts.

8. Respect the Opinions of Others

Not everyone sees the world the same way; in fact, no one does. When five people witness an auto accident, police compile five different reports. Each opinion is based on an individual viewpoint. That's why there are 5 billion people in the world, not one very big person.

Other team members may come up with ideas that you think are the craziest things you've ever heard uttered by another human being. That doesn't make them crazy or deserving of disrespect because their opinions differ from yours. The best teams are made up of people with the biggest diversity of perceptions, who first learn to understand and value the opinions and views of others.

Trust without respect is like a sandwich without bread.

If you don't or can't respect someone, especially on your team, you will never trust them. People do not come equipped with RESPECT buttons they can push, and thereby be flooded with respect for others. Indeed, we are stingy with respect: "I can't give it; they have to earn it."

If you feel swamped by your own stinginess, what can you do? First, acknowledge the fact, and concede that it is as least partially your problem. Everyone deserves a basic level of respect. After all, if your nature makes you contemptuous of even that basic level, you may be all of the problem.

Hint: people who lack respect for others don't always have the abundance of self-esteem that they think they have.

To learn respect, return to the fundamentals of goals and roles. Focus on the task, not the personnel. Try to build a narrow basis for trust on what a person commits to and does—being a good soldier. Set aside past bad behaviors or personality quirks.

Gossip kills respect. Often you will get advance word from the grapevine to "watch out for Charlie." Charlie's reputation isn't Charlie. Form your opinions about him by working with him, not from the vague rumblings of the lunchroom.

9. Empower Team Members to Act

Team members cannot be empowered to act; they must empower themselves. As a team member, however, you can help create an atmosphere in which other team members feel free to take risks, and to take action towards the completion of tasks.

In an organization where people are afraid to take risks or action without first checking with some higher authority, they will resist any attempts to "empower" them. Where team members do feel comfortable initiating action and letting their boss know what's going on (so the boss doesn't wind up with a face full of egg), trust starts to grow.

Trust given results in trust, support, and loyalty in return.

Perceptions and Trust

A few paragraphs ago—in number 8, "Respect the Opinions of Others"—we talked about how different people can view the same situation in different ways, and arrive at conflicting interpretations. Obviously, when people are seeing the same thing in different ways, they start to wonder about one another. "Is he crazy?" "She is really deluding herself!" "Do I dare share my opinions with people who can't see the nose in front of their own faces?"

Perceptual differences between team members are a major cause of trust breakdown. To reverse this breakdown, we must first understand that our perceptions of the world differ for good reasons. We all *select, organize,* and *interpret* information differently. Let's talk about each one in turn.

Perceptions are **selected.** We are all of us constantly surrounded and bombarded by activity. Lights, noise, talking, wind, and even our own thinking are sources of stimulation that we can perceive.

To make sense out of all this stuff, we become selective in our perceptions. We edit. We block out the buzzing lights, the air conditioner hum, the noisy conversations, and the child asking for our help—and concentrate on what we are reading. When the child finally does get our attention, we refocus, block out the rest, swivel toward the child like Robocop and say, "Sorry, I didn't hear you."

We select the stimulation that we wish to perceive, based on our *expectations,* our *needs,* and our *wants.* If our first impression of someone is negative ("She sure dresses like a slob"), we tend to pick out subsequent actions that support those first impressions ("Get a load of that desk"). We expect certain things to be true and sure enough, we find them. Nothing is easier than corroborating our prejudices.

If we need more office space, we notice all the vacant space in the building—space we never noticed before. If we want a new boat, all of a sudden we become aware of all the boats for sale along the road on our way home from work.

The most powerful word in the English language is the word NOTICE. If you don't notice your environment, you can't interact effectively with it.

Once we've selected information, we **organize** it via two very interesting methods. One is called *figure-ground.* That is, one set of information becomes the figure we focus on and everything else becomes the ignored background. Figure-ground occurs when two people think they're talking about the same thing, but actually are talking about two different things.

Maybe it's happened to you. You're in a conversation with someone. The conversation ends; you think you have agreement. Then fifteen minutes later, you stop, slap yourself on the forehead, and ask yourself, "Were we even talking about the same thing?"

Perhaps you noticed the other person doing something totally different from what you thought you had agreed to. In reality, you both heard different things from the same conversation based upon each person's predetermined focus or priority. Each was listening to their "inner ear," rather than to what the other person was saying. The conversation foundered on the shoals of each side's self-fascination. The conversation was nothing but a "dual-monologue." It could not progress to true communication.

What's important to us may not be what's important to someone else.

That's where many misunderstandings begin. To stop this sort of misunderstanding, never end a conversation without first clarifying *who* is responsible for *what* by *when,* and *how* you are going to check with each other to make sure you're on track.

The second way we organize information is through *closure.* Closure is based on the principle that where there's smoke, there's fire. If we have incomplete information about something, we tend to fill in the blanks using what we already do know. (Smoke, therefore fire.)

The problem is, we have a natural tendency to fill in the blanks with *negatives,* not positives. So if we get left out of a meeting or off a memo we feel we should have received, we feel the sender intentionally tried to do us harm. Sound familiar? The higher the trust levels, the less likely negative closure will occur.

Many times we see only a part of what is going on, but we organize it by filling in what is missing. The parts we fill in are as real to us as that which we have actually observed. This is why rumors are so easy to start, so powerful once they have started, and so hard to put an end to. The best way to overcome this tendency is to check out the facts or ask for the other person's intentions the next time you start feeling upset about what someone is communicating to you.

When we assume negative intentions on the part of others, we react by "getting even."

The next step, after we have selected and organized information, is to **interpret** it. Our interpretations are affected by the ambiguity of the situation, our attitude, our orientation, and the psychological context of the situation.

Ambiguity

A man dashes into an airport bar in an obvious hurry, orders a drink, slams it down, throws a $5 bill on the bar, and runs out. The bartender slowly walks up to the bar, picks up the money, turns to another patron and says, "Isn't that interesting. He was in such a hurry, he forgot to pay for his drink . . . but he left me a $5 tip."

Ambiguity. If you don't tell another person how you want them to interpret your information, they're free to interpret it based on whatever happens to be rumbling around in their brain at the time.

Attitude

If you're like most normal people, your mood changes during the day based upon your interactions with other people or information. You may know what your attitude is at the time, but others don't. In order to enhance your communications with others, since they are interpreting your messages based upon both your verbal and nonverbal behaviors, you need to let them know what your attitude is at the time of your conversation. Some people have taken a 4"× 4" piece of cardboard and drawn a "Mr. Happy" face on one side, a "Mr. Yuk" face on the other, and hung it outside their work space. As their mood changes during the day, they flip the card back and forth. This helps those coming in to talk to better interpret the information they receive.

How things look on the outside of us depends a lot on how things are on the inside of us.

Orientation

We all have orientations or comfort zones in which we operate. These orientations may be made up of our experiences from where we grew up (New York, Peoria, Hong Kong, etc.), our religious/

philosophical backgrounds (Jewish, Catholic, Lutheran, Humanist, Muslim, Atheist, etc.), our education and occupation (MBA, Ph.D., engineer, writer, salesperson, etc.), our cultural heritage (Italian-American, African-American, Latin-American, Native-American, etc.), our color charts (black, white, brown, red, yellow, green, puce, etc.), sexual preferences (heterosexual, homosexual, both, neither, etc.). Our orientation is unique and makes us who we are. It also requires us to be sensitive to the orientations of others if we are to communicate more effectively with them.

Psychological Context

This is a natural human trap in which we often get caught. Basically, we all interpret information we hear based on the last piece of information we happened to be thinking about. For example, if a salesperson is thinking she knows what a customer needs ("blue coat"), she may unthinkingly ring up the blue coat—even though the customer only bought a pair of red socks. The salesperson wrote the order based on what she was thinking, not on what she actually heard.

In factories there is a storage space set aside at the end of the assembly line. It's called the redo line, because it's where everything that has to be redone is put. It has been estimated that 40 percent of the cost of redoing work, across all industries, is the result of mistakes incurred because of psychological context—people misperceiving, seeing false patterns, unthinkingly turning a screw to the left instead of the right. We slap ourselves on the forehead when we make these completely avoidable mistakes—then we proceed to make them again.

The lesson here is that team members must be vigilant about their own attitudes. Suspicions that would have saved us from treachery and defenestration in another era become our workaday enemy in the team era. We must learn to identify when our instincts about one another are serving us well, and when they are doing us a disservice.

It's OK to trust your senses. It's your brain you have to keep an eye on.

Trust depleted may never be regained. It is a tough business—two strikes and you're out. When trust is gone, it must be replaced by control: rules, regulations, structure, three-ring notebooks. The team spends as much time policing itself as doing its job.

A world without trust is a world full of . . . lawyers. Lawyers are how our society imposes control in the absence of trust. They weigh us down with structure and penalties. They create language that is frightfully clear, and frighteningly uncreative. The irony is that control ultimately fails to control—for who can really understand the clarity of legalese? A team that comes up empty in the trust department will start to think like a lawyer—not what works, or what is best, or what meets the customer's needs, but what technically complies with what is asked of us.

A final disturbing thought: While a team leader can take heroic measures to regain trust—submitting to a public whipping is one promising avenue, apologizing is another—there is precious little that rank and file team members can do. But here and there, even in the darkest organizations, there are always good people who speak the truth, and devil take the hindmost.

Even hell has its beloved trustees—old cons who have done hard time, who know the ropes, and retain a measure of grizzled humanity. Their humanity is expressed as a Dilbert cartoon on the cubicle wall. They are saying that, all you can do, when you know you are in hell, is laugh about it.

chapter 19

Change Issues

We are passing through an era of reinvention, reengineering, and transformation. And we hate it.

We hate change because no matter which of three classic responses we make to it, it wins. If we don't *embrace change,* it overtakes us and hurts like hell. If we do try to embrace it, it still knocks us for a loop. If we try to *anticipate change* and be ready when it appears—well, it doesn't make much difference, we still wind up on our keesters. Change is pain, even when self-administered.

Change is to a team as the ocean is to a sponge—it is inside, outside, everywhere, the milieu in which everything happens. In most companies, teams are a *part* of the change. Because teams are geared toward flexibility, they should be better able to deal with the difficulties of change than conventional work groups.

But it's still a drag, and many, many teams have perished because they could not adapt to the changes engulfing them. This chapter looks at the ways change can batter a team, and the ways teams can fight back.

Understanding Change

There's not much we could tell an acquaintance of ours, Steve. He and his team were hit hard by change, and it extracted a terrible toll.

He had to move his product design team from a remote location to headquarters (some 20 miles away) while the manufacturing group they supported remained behind. This move didn't make sense to most of the team. The fact that the decision came both as a surprise and with short notice caused some anxiety and tension. Steve's challenge was fourfold: to take the edge off his team's stress, to weave himself and the team into the new surroundings, to not lose touch with manufacturing, 20 miles away, and to maintain performance while all this was happening.

There were many decisions to make and many people to contact in order to get stuff done. It meant setting up in a very short time a functioning equivalent of work processes that had taken years to get right at the old location. Considerations included supplies, copying, mail, carpools, parking, communication strategies, policies, procedures, name badges, space allocation—and where did you say the bathrooms were?

It took Steve three months and several economy-size jars of Excedrin to overcome the team's initial resistance, make the dreaded move, and settle down to business. Three months of pushing and pulling with various headquarters staffers who pretended he had just arrived from Mars ("And you are who, you're here to do what?") Three months of tension, confusion, fidgetiness, frustration, hard feelings.

How did productivity fare through this disaster? Superbly,—not!

By the end of their ordeal, which the team endured with fortitude and resilience, they were wrecks—demoralized, exhausted, and vulnerable. And of course there was no rest period for them, because change never lets up. One wave engulfs you, and its big sister is coming up behind.

Seven Hard Truths

If you are serious about helping your team and its members increase their tolerance for change, there are seven facts about people and change that you must understand.

When undergoing change:

1. *People feel awkward, ill-at-ease, and self-conscious.* The people best adapted to change are those raised in an ever-changing environment, like army brats who move every three or so years, or research scientists seeking change with every breath. For the rest of us, change is scary, painful, and unwanted.

2. *People will think first about what they must give up.* It's a defense mechanism, the worst-case scenario. Team members will first think about what they have to lose by being on a team rather than what they have to gain. The job of an effective team leader, then, becomes one of painting positive expectations of outcomes to overcome this natural defensive behavior.

3. *People will feel alone.* Most people will not share their feelings of change anxiety with other team members for fear of being seen as uncertain or uncommitted. As a result, little communication occurs during the very time when good communication is most critical. During change, the tendency is to hunker down and stiffen the upper lip, all the while feeling isolated and alone. And when it comes to change, feelings are facts. Now is the moment to have team members get their feelings out on the table and resolved.

4. *People can handle only so much change.* We've worked with several organizations during major change times—some more successful than others. One of the keys to successful change is timing. Companies that dole out change in small doses over longer periods of time, hoping to minimize negative impact, are surprised at the sudden dip in morale after about the second or third dose. Even medicine given in small doses loses impact in short order.

Until team members can picture in their minds what their tasks and their roles will be like when this change is complete, they will probably just nod their heads and not comply. Organizations that have had the best success with change make major steps in short timeframes, with the end product carefully described up front. With this information under their belt, team members tolerate the short-term pain for the longer-term payoff. The "dribble" or incremental change method only heightens the sense of mistrust of management that many employees already have.

5. *People have different readiness levels for change.* Any time a team is asked to change, some members will be excited and ready, and others will appear to have anchors tied around their enthusiasm. As we saw in Chapter 10 ("The People Problem"), people are very different from one another. How fast they can commit to change is just another way in which we differ. The challenge for teams is to boost the readiness of their least-ready members, because these people determine the pace of the team as a whole. Any attempt to push faster will meet with increased resistance and slow the process. Following the steps laid out later in this chapter will help speed the change process along, even for the less enthusiastic.

6. *People will fret that they don't have enough resources.* The first noise you hear from people in change pain is, "We could do it if we only had more resources." Sure, we all would like additional resources—but we usually have not made much use of the resources already at our disposal. Untapped, available, shared, borrowed, stolen, or heretofore unknown resources are usually all a team needs to get through a tough change phase. Look around. Use the unused and underused. Make do. Or don't do. One nifty trick, after you've exhausted your search, is to go to the persons blocking the needed resources and ask for their input on alternative resources. Those who block usually know the way around the block, if anyone bothers to ask. They won't volunteer this information, but if asked, they'll usually tell.

7. *If you take the pressure off, people will revert to their old behaviors.* Momentum is an amazing and wonderful force. Like a compass, it keeps you going in the same direction. If the direction you're going, however, is the wrong one and needs changing, momentum can kill you. Momentum, like a magnet, will pull you back in the old direction, the old way of doing things. Change is a temporary force that pulls you in a new direction; but only if it's applied continuously until the new behaviors become the norm, the new north. If you take the pressure off too early in a change process, the team will revert to the old way of doing business, old relationships, old behaviors, old processes, old habits.

Change and Personality

Personality type naturally plays a role in one's ability to meet change head on.

You remember the grid showing Analyticals, Drivers, Expressives, and Amiables.

The same grid, with a little change, tells a story about change potentials:

(metamoron)			(metaphile)
	ANALYTICAL	DRIVER	
	AMIABLE	EXPRESSIVE	
(metaphobe)			(metamaniac)

Each type is perfectly capable of normal change. The center of the grid could be shaded in as "OK about change." At their extreme edges, however—like when a Driver is a very strong Driver, or an Analytical is a super-Analytical—pronounced differences become apparent.

▶ *Drivers* love to lead, and true leading implies change, so it is logical that Drivers have a special knack for changing. Pure Drivers are *metaphiles,* cheerful embracers of the new and untested.

▶ *Expressives* like to play. Their natural mode is exploration, and that is an intrinsically useful part of change. Pure Expressives are *metamaniacs,* so enamored of change that they have to be changing in order to function.

▶ *Amiables* are the people everyone else loves to have around. They are the perfect antidote in a marriage to a strong Driver— they smile, they shrug, they love, they forgive. Not exactly hard chargers. Thus Amiables have a tendency to be *metaphobes,* people disinclined by nature to enjoy change much.

▶ *Analyticals* are usually right, but they can be awfully tight about it. They are the perfectionists of the world, dotting every *i* and crossing every *t.* At the extreme, they become *metamorons,* people to whom change is completely unacceptable—because change ruins their data, their level thinking field.

What does it mean?

It means you don't load a change initiative team with metamaniacs—there will be hamburger all over the highway. Neither do you assign a metamoron the task of leading a team in a pilot change project.

Most teams contain people from more than one group. This is not a bad thing. A team with a metaphile on it will likely galvanize everyone else to follow. A team with a metamaniac on it will benefit from the reassuring foot-dragging effect of a metaphobe.

As always, the beauty of teams is the diversity of their members. A team of all metamorons—all people with a strong Analytical bent, like a lot of functional teams in finance, engineering, and the other analytical arts—is going to have a hell of a time moving off the dime.

By the way, in our practice, we have learned that not many people enjoy being called metamorons. Just remember that only extreme, off-the-chart Analyticals qualify for this august title. Chances are, you're much too balanced to deserve such an epithet.

Human Speedbumps

The most constant factor in each of our lives is change. At work, at home, at play, daily transitions occur that make things different. Some variations are large and significant; most are small and simply intrude upon our daily routine. In order to understand our reaction to change, we first need to look at the *speedbumps* which slow us down as we approach any change. These fall into three types: *People, Processes,* and *Structures.*

Resistance to change is almost a fundamental fact of human nature. We wish this were not true. Resistance to the inevitable suggests there is something sort of stupid about us. But true it is.

The sequence goes like this:

1. Unplanned change creates anxiety . . .

2. Anxiety drags its feet in resistance . . .

3. Irresistible force collides with immovable object . . .

4. Team explodes in immense fireball.

It happens every time. Well, not every time. Few lottery winners decline to take possession of their winnings, to sidestep the changes that wealth brings. But most change stimulates resistance.

Human beings are creatures of habit, each one surrounded by an individual *comfort zone* of behaviors and interactions. Too much variation often means we must leave our comfort zone and face unknown consequences, which we then have to evaluate.

If we win the lottery, get a promotion, or find a new friend, most of us react positively. It's where we perceive negative consequences to change, or continued uncertainty, that we resist.

Resistance can come from a number of sources:

▶ *Fear* . . . of failure; of loss (loss of identity, belonging, control, meaning, security, etc.); of the unknown; and of negative consequences, such as criticism for mistakes.

▶ *Laziness* . . . not wanting to put in the effort to make the change happen. These are the people who only see the short-term work required and become myopic to the big picture or future, long-term gain.

▶ *Previous momentum* . . . too much time and effort expended in the "old ways." This is the opposite of laziness. One is heading deliberately in a familiar direction, has picked up speed, is feeling OK—then is asked to apply the brakes and turn in a brand-new direction. This takes a toll on renewed team commitment, not to mention brake lining.

▶ *History* . . . dislike or distrust of the initiators of change. This is where "getting even" sometimes takes place. Either to settle an old score or just because you don't like the person in charge, you resist—actively or passively.

▶ *Payoff* . . . no perceived return for your change investment (*What's in it for me?*). Not only are humans creatures of habit, but we're a bit selfish too. If we do not see an advantage for ourselves in the change effort, we tend to wait out the change or not participate with enthusiasm. It becomes the task of the leaders within an organization to clarify the payoff for each individual team member, as appropriate.

Process Speedbumps

We keep an eye out for process speedbumps, so they don't bounce us off the road to effective change. These include poor planning and communication, as well as poor follow-through and follow-up.

Planning and communication run hand in hand. You may have

the best-thought-out plans around, but if no one knows about and buys into them, they're useless. Similarly, communication pipelines, either formal or informal, are just that—pipe. Whether they are used as sewers or rocket launchers is up to you.

Another potential process speedbump involves poor (or lack of) follow-through and follow-up. To become real a vision requires action. Just because you learned new skills in class, or talked about changing something at work, won't make change happen unless there is a built-in process for following through on action plans and checking progress (follow-up) at predetermined times down the road. This helps folks keep from falling back into their old habits of behavior and performance.

Structure Speedbumps

Has anyone ever said to you, "You can't get there from here," or quoted policies, procedures, rules, or regulations as reasons why something can't be changed? If so, you experienced a structural speedbump. Most policies and procedures (see Chapter 9, The Wrong Policies and Procedures) were created for specific reasons, at a time in the past. Very rarely are they reexamined in the light of either current events or future goals and modified as necessary. Instead of being cast in Jell-O as was their intent, they're usually chiseled in stone. People come and people go, but stupid rules are forever. Modifying or moving around these speedbumps requires a careful mixture of Vaseline and dynamite.

Rules for Team Change

We hereby decree twelve key rules for reducing team resistance and clearing the way for effective team change:

1. *Plan for change.*

2. *Involve others in the change process; get stakeholder agreement and commitment.*

3. *Communicate, communicate, communicate.*

4. *Generate expectations of outcomes.*

5. *Create influence/support networks.*

6. *Obtain adequate resources.*

7. *Generate critical mass to create and maintain momentum.*

8. *Follow through and follow up.*

9. *Persist, and be ready to pay the price for change—mistakes.*

10. *Reinforce early and often.*

11. *Keep processes and techniques simple.*

12. *Lead the way.*

Let's look at each rule in turn, and explain why it warrants the imperial mandate.

Plan for Change

We plan for change in order to have some measure of influence over it. We want to have a say in *where we're going* and *what we are going to become.*

These are the 13 questions team members must ask as they plan for change:

1. What are our goals, objectives, and strategies?

2. How do they tie into the larger mission?

3. What resources do we anticipate needing—human, dollar, etc.?

4. What is our implementation schedule?

5. Who must be involved in formulating the change plan? How? When?

6. What is the desired consequence of each change step?

7. How will we know we've been successful? Can we give examples of desired outcomes?

8. When will each change step be completed?

9. What alternative strategies can we implement if "Plan A" fails?

10. How will we deal with unanticipated events?

11. Who needs to be influenced?

12. Who will be involved in the implementation plan? How? When?

13. Who might we use as blockers? How can we bring them on board?

As you can see, planning requires the gathering of a great deal of information from lots of people. The process of this data gathering has three effects on your immediate team:

1. it involves them;

2. it builds up an expectation for change; and

3. it enhances their trust in the process because they can see it happening.

The problem is that once this planning process has begun, so has the ticking of the clocks inside the heads of team members who wait impatiently to see tangible change outcomes. Ticking raises stress, so continuous communication becomes crucial at this point.

Involve Others in the Change Process; Get Stakeholder Agreement and Commitment

People don't usually resist *positive* change. We *like* winning the Publisher's Clearinghouse Sweepstakes. It's negative change—having to fend off a band of marauding baboons, or having to learn Chinese in a plummeting elevator—that puts us off our feed.

To reduce resistance, try moving the change out of the shadows of negativity and into the light of day. Encourage team members to participate as partners in the change, and reward them when they do. Resistance will drop and commitment should increase.

Participation can be active, directly involved in asking and answering the questions above. For example, bringing problems to the group and soliciting their inputs on possible solutions tends to overcome many negative expectations of change. Or participation can be passive, simply receiving continuous communication and feedback on the process.

The most important aspect of involvement, however, is getting people oriented toward the future, helping them anticipate and embrace future outcomes. Determine all the stakeholders in any change and try to reach an agreement on "what is a desirable outcome?"

What will that outcome look, feel, taste, and smell like? Is it OK? The pathways of change toward the future have many twists, turns, and off-ramps. Encouraging people to help be the *drivers* of the change vehicle (determining what maps to use, what off ramps to take) builds a commitment to the outcomes of change. It also allows them to move within their comfort zones—to keep the process moving forward. In other words, it makes the change *their* change.

Communicate, Communicate, Communicate

Because human beings are such creatures of habit, taking them in a new direction or even improving their lot by providing them with "better" processes or enhanced information tends to make them a bit skittish.

Surprises especially build anxiety!

It's often not the *content* of change that people resist, as much as the *process* of providing it to them. Even if the outcome of the change is eventually positive, people may resist if they do not feel communicated with from the beginning. Effective changework demands continuous communication—before, during, and after the change process. This communication includes anticipating and answering questions like:

▶ If this is our vision, how do we plan to get from here to there?

▶ What is involved in this change process?

▶ Who will be involved and how?

▶ When can we expect to see results?

▶ How can we be kept informed of progress?

▶ How does all this affect me personally?

Use multiple channels of communication to answer and update individuals so they feel less a victim of, and more an active participant in the change process. Examples of multiple channels include internal newsletters, notes placed in pay envelopes, small and large open discussion meetings, ad hoc committees, informal networks, and grapevines.

One technique is to place large whiteboards in hallways, where people can express their views and sentiments. This provides a forum for folks to express their concerns and issues, to clarify payoffs, and to provide inputs and alternative solutions and ideas. If it is not practical to involve all those affected, involve a representative sample—like a focus group—and provide a means to explain the *range and reason* for changes to everyone else.

Generate Expectations of Outcomes

People have an interesting internal process that tries to match up what we *actually* see in our environment with what we *expected* to see. We pick out only those things that help us meet our expectations, and screen out the rest.

If you can create a positive expectation for change, or help folks see what any change will look like after it has taken place, they will feel safer and more secure when the change actually happens. They will also push harder to make sure that the change *does* take place, and that it looks like what it was expected to look like.

Create Influence/Support Networks

Another element of successful changework is influence/support networks. You cannot create a successful change in a vacuum. Whether formal or informal, networks create both checkpoints and anxiety relievers for any change. Questions to ask:

▶ Are we heading in the right direction?

▶ What modifications, if any, do we need to make in terms of people, processes, structures, resources, schedules, outcomes, commitment, etc.?

▶ Is anyone feeling a pinch about the change progress or direction to date?

Change usually causes one's comfort zone to shrink. But you can minimize shrinkage by expanding the support network and encouraging frequent use of it. Support can come from multiple sources (bosses, coworkers, mentors, subordinates, associates, cross-functional support teams, etc.). The more, the merrier.

Support networks have broader uses than just easing of personal anxiety. They can be used as *points of influence* to make change happen. This is where strategically placed *change advocates* can make a real difference. These "change agents" are people of influence—formal or informal—who advocate for change within your organization. Selling the need for and the rationale behind any change efforts to these people allows them to pave the way within their circles of influence.

Also, getting opinion-makers on your side makes it easier to sell any change to a larger group of people in a shorter period of time. Ultimately, these folks will help make or break any significant change effort anyway—so why not get them actively involved in the process early?

Obtain Adequate Resources

Ask for help obtaining the amount of human and capital resources necessary to create and sustain any positive change. You may not get it, but you'll have tried. The research is very compelling on this point—many more actual requisitions are granted than non-requisitions.

Another benefit of asking and being turned down is that you may learn why the request was not granted, which is good information to have for the next request.

Generate Critical Mass to Create and Maintain Momentum

Be aware of the number of people necessary to successfully carry off your change process. Two out of ten won't cut it. You need a broad base—unanimous within the team, and a healthy number of advocates, champions, and friends on the outside.

Once the change effort achieves momentum, use this movement as the impetus for longer lasting or broader impact.

Follow Through and Follow Up

The best-laid plans of mice and men can go down the tube in a hurry if you are not on top of any change process. The process of follow-through and follow-up should be viewed not as a *policing* function, but a coaching one.

Many people have habits or concerns that can get in the way of making changes. The coaching process allows you and them to identify both personal and work-related barriers to change as they are being experienced and talk about ways to address them.

Follow-up can take place at either predetermined times (once a week, month, quarter, etc.), or when people reach predetermined stages in the change process (as when the phones are about to be installed).

Persist, and Be Ready to Pay the Price for Change—Mistakes

Change means risk. Risk means mistakes. Fear of punishment for mistakes encourages "CYA" and reduces the willingness to take the risks necessary to make change work.

Recently, a CEO of a major international manufacturing company made this point to us by relating a story from within his organization. Several members of the engineering department came to him with an idea for a "better" process for making a certain component. It involved both new technology and a different process. It was a bit costly, but they were sure it would pay off in the long haul.

Having been delegated the responsibility and authority to make a decision, they did. The new process failed miserably. Several weeks later the CEO called these engineers into his office. They thought they were going to get punished for their failure. To their surprise, the CEO had canned hams waiting for them. In astonishment, they asked for an explanation.

He responded that just because the outcome was less than expected, that did not mean their decision was wrong. The only failure would have been *not* to try new and different approaches; for, as he noted, innovation would be the hallmark of all their future success. (The canned hams idea came from David Letterman.)

The failure was a short-term "hit" to the company, but a long-term payoff in terms of unleashed creativity and willingness to change.

Reinforce Early and Often

Being creatures of habit, it is impossible for us to completely abandon the "old ways" for the "new way" overnight. Change does move people and organizations toward desired outcomes—but slowly, in measurable steps.

The grease that keeps the change process going in a consistent direction is *positive reinforcement*. A word of acknowledgement, a formal recognition, a pat on the back—all count as reinforcement. The ideal reinforcement is the one that motivates an individual employee for the progress he or she is making.

Reinforcement need not wait for completed outcomes. Ideally it is built into the process, and awarded for *progress towards outcomes*. Public reinforcement of small changes, especially early on, creates the momentum necessary to reach the desired goals.

Keep Processes and Techniques Simple

The fashion is to say that complex problems require complex solutions. Maybe. But solutions that throw a team into an uproar, that take people too far out of their comfort zones or are too technical, will result in great resistance. Like eating an elephant, complex change must be accomplished one bite at a time.

Lead the Way

Finally, the importance of leadership to successful changework cannot be overemphasized. Effective leadership is a must for effective organizational change. We have already mentioned the coaching function of leadership. There are several other requirements, two of which involve *vision* and *pathway*.

Vision provides a dream of the future—what your organization will look like down the road. Pathway provides some sense of how you expect to get from here to there, as well as the impact on people, processes, and structures involved. Providing a way of determining the pathway to achieving your organization's future creates a lifeline for people to grasp while they are accomplishing changework.

The leadership keys to positive outcomes include *attitude, analysis,* and *action.* One of the sharpest arrows in a leader's quiver is a *positive attitude* toward innovation and change. Attitude *sets the stage* as leaders attempt to energize others.

Creating an expectation for change as the norm for all employees (especially new hires) allows change to be seen as part of the everyday process of conducting business. For example, companies like 3M have created a norm of having a large percentage of their products produced from technologies that are not more than five years old. This stipulation creates an atmosphere supportive of continuous innovation and change, and guards against the bad habits encouraged by "cash cow" operations.

Next, ongoing analysis of progress toward outcomes, along with feedback from all those involved in creating change, keeps people fired up and on the right track. Finally, when leaders take personal responsibility to make small *action* steps happen, the entire organization becomes sharper.

Leveraging Your Change

The emphasis on change in this chapter may lull you into thinking that change itself is the goal of teams. It isn't. Change, whether for good or for ill, is the environment teams work within. Good change, or improvement in the goals, processes, and output of a team, is the result of competent change management. There are several tools we can recommend for the effective leveraging of change.

Action Forums

As part of the increased communication required during periods of change, groups of individuals impacted by any specific change suggestion are gathered into *action forums*. These groups go through a discovery and bargaining process, where they discuss the impact of the change on each individual, how to minimize any potential negative impact, what barriers need to be crossed, and how they can help make the change a reality.

Pilot Projects

The creation of a *trial balloon*—a tryout—is sometimes necessary to see what the impact of any change will be. Using small groups of enthusiastic people to discover real outcomes, before launching widespread change, provides a low-cost, reduced-risk snapshot of what will happen.

What-If Scenarios

We have made the point before that the keys to successful change include persistent analysis and action. Your pilot project may be on the success road, but how are you going to monitor and adjust your change strategies as you encounter unplanned variables?

We know of a football coach who once created a training program called the "Burma Road." The running back's task was to charge quickly up a field full of movable blocking dummies. One never knew how the dummies would react to the running back's approach—some would move toward him violently, some would move to the side, some would pull away, etc. The effect of this drill was to build a sense of anticipation and agility.

Building a Burma Road in an organization undergoing change means creating an ongoing process of assessment—monitoring, checking, analyzing your progress and your impact, anticipating the unplanned, and fostering agility by dreaming up *what-if* scenarios.

Dodge the Potholes

The road to effective change is strewn with potholes, any one of which can throw your efforts out of alignment with your goals. In order for your organization and the people in it to have positive outcomes and build an "edge," it is important to *do change right*.

Consider following the twelve rules for change to achieve the commitment, momentum, and success your organization deserves. Your team's underbody will thank you.

part three

Team Myths

▼

chapter 20

The Myth of Adventure Learning

Rays of light spire over the humpback mountain peak, breaking up the blue sky. Christine stands facing the light, on the tip of a rock promontory, 70 feet over a pitted gorge leading down another 500 feet to a winding canyon stream. Falling means instant death.

As she greets the morning, the breeze blowing through her hair, she lifts her arms, teeters, and falls gently backward—into the arms of twelve team members, waiting just below.

Then the group trudges to the next adventure site, a pole Christine must climb in order to overcome her fears. Her twelve teammates will be belaying her with support ropes all the way. When the day is done, everyone who climbed will be awarded an ornamental carabiner, to put on the desk back at the office as a paperweight and a permanent reminder of the important lessons about teamwork learned up on the windswept slopes of Mount Cooperation.

Welcome to the heart-pounding, high-fiving world of adventure learning.

Adventure learning is a group event in which a team is put through a series of challenging physical and mental tasks. They often take place outdoors in an idyllic setting, at a retreat in the mountains, or a dude ranch, or a park. They are facilitator led, and they build on the psychological lessons learned years ago in the 1970s, in Carl Rogers-style encounter groups.

Back then it was discovered that people could experience sensational breakthroughs in behavior if asked to do things they do not ordinarily do, with the rest of the group acting as support. The classic example is "Trust Falls." In this exercise you put a blindfolded person on a table, then let them fall backward, with the other group members catching the falling individual.

There are two basic degrees of adventure learning, higher risk and lower risk; we'll call them "high ropes" and "low ropes." High ropes is the more adventurous of the two. It involves climbing mountains, crossing rope bridges, rapid descents on pulleys, and the like. There is some degree of actual physical danger in high ropes exercises—your teammates could decide not to belay you with their support ropes, and you could fall off the mountain.

Low ropes involve very little actual risk. It is adventure learning on a budget, usually a series of physical outdoor exercises that can be done in a park or backyard. They often begin with something like the Druid's Knot. Team members form a circle and then, taking turns, clasp right hands with the right hand of someone else in the circle. Then they do the same thing with their left hand. People are pulled very close with all the handshakes. The objective now is for everyone to untangle the knot, without letting go.

Usually the people most engaged in the solution are in the greatest pain, their bodies contorted like pretzels. Eventually they have all disentangled themselves and they form a large ring, much bigger than the original circle. From a knot to a ring: confusion to order—get it?

There sometimes comes a moment when the group simply can't figure out how to disengage without some people letting go. When this happens, those who let go become "blind." They must close their eyes and be guided from that point on by other team members—even into the next exercise! This is seen as a good team-building behavior—those with information assisting those without information.

(Some team "leaders" volunteer *others* as a sacrifice for the team good. "Igor, you let go now." An optimized team does not command team members to die for it; it does not even ask for volunteers.)

The next exercise may be the Spider's Web. This is done outside. A very long rope is strung between a tree, and then, through a series of loopbacks, is formed into a giant, semicircular spider's web. The strands of the web form perhaps 20 "windows," rather like the zones on a dartboard. The team challenge is to get every member of the team through the windows without disturbing the ropes. Two corollary rules make it even harder: no window can be used more than once, and some of the players will be "blind" from the previous exercise and must be helped through, blindfolded. If you touch the web, you become blind.

Another low-ropes exercise example is called Acid River. The team must cross a raging imaginary river of acid. They have a dozen cinder blocks and three or four 4 × 4 planks. Using the planks, they can make bridges from block to block—but there are not enough planks to make a complete walkway to safety, so the planks have to be carefully moved back and forth as each person, small group, or team makes the treacherous crossing. Again, the exercise inherits however many people went "blind" from the previous exercise—and anyone stepping off the boards goes blind.

(We have seen games in which everyone is blind by the end. It is a very pathetic sight, grown men and women groping for a board that is right in front of them—the blind leading the blind, teammates to the corrosive end. It is distressing and wonderful by turns.)

These games are, first and foremost, a lot of fun to play. Most new teams are pretty stiff and formal with one another. They have never met outside the work situation. These games help break the ice, and get people physically involved with one another. We are talking group intimacy here, and there are moments that will strike those whose noses are blue-hued as risqué, a sort of company-sanctioned Twister.

The lessons people learn in these groups include overcoming fear, overcoming distrust, and the synergistic power of a group working to support the individual. People who do this rave about it. They say it enabled them to do things they could never do. They say it changed their lives. Afterwards there is much hugging, exulting, and people saying, "Why didn't we do this years ago?"

Everyone is ecstatic, certain that the lessons of teamwork will naturally translate to something wonderful once they get back to the office.

But . . . when the team folds up its ropes and packs away its carabiners and heads back to the city, are they a better team?

In our experience, they are not. People may be friendlier. They may feel that they got to know one another, outside of the work setting. They may feel lots of good warm fuzzies toward one another—which is good. They may head back with better intentions to team with one another—also good.

But they will not be a better team, because the mountaineering or web-climbing exercises were not really about teaming. These activities were not developed to improve teamwork. They were developed to explore various dimensions of personal development. They are fantastic for achieving personal breakthroughs with one's own demons and fears. And yes, they are very good at improving one's personal attitudes about being in groups, and allowing oneself to trust others.

But teams are not failing because people have fears and phobias, or are unable, in a broad generic way, to "trust." Teams are failing because members are confused about what their roles are, what their mission is, and whether or not they have the authority to do whatever needs to be done. Their trust issues are specific to roles and procedures—not to one another's willingness to catch them when they fall.

All this stuff with the carabiners and pulleys is great fun, and personally exhilarating, but pointless. Training firms that sell adventure learning for the personal exploration benefits are giving you your money's worth. Training firms that sell adventure learning for the teambuilding benefits are selling you a bill of goods.

You know the carabiner paperweights you get when you graduate from a high-ropes routine? We know someone with three of them on her credenza. Last time we saw her, she was heading up the mountain again, for a fourth. "It's such a powerful experience," she says.

So why does her team have to keep going back?

"Oh, we've got problems."

The Myth that Sports Teams and Work Teams Are Similar

P eople who like pro sports have a special disadvantage in team building: they expect the process to mirror their favorite sports team.

This expectation nearly always fails, and is especially unpleasant for other team members who don't happen to follow pro sports. Posting action pictures of Michael Jordan or Randy Moss or Picabo Street, in hopes of engendering feelings of healthy competition and stellar performance, just doesn't connect for everyone. But try explaining that to sports fans.

This disconnect was brought home to us by the publication a couple of years ago of *Everyone's a Coach,* a collaboration between Ken (*One-Minute Manager*) Blanchard and Don Shula, Hall of Fame coach of the Miami Dolphins football team.

We love Ken Blanchard, and we admire Coach Shula. And the book is harmless enough, a melange of inspiring sports stories and happy team talk.

But then *USA Today* interviewed us for an article on the book, and the analogy between coaching pro sports teams and ordinary work teams. The paper wanted us to endorse the concept. Based on our experiences with teams, we couldn't do it.

Sports teams at the professional level are not quite teams in the sense that we use the word. They are really entertainment teams, and they perform very well under enormous stress. But there's little carryover to our kind of teams.

True, sports teams are groups of people with selected areas of expertise, who share a common goal (winning). But they are led the old-fashioned way, by a supervisor/coach, who is above them in a hierarchy.

Try to imagine a "self-directed" sports team. A self-directed sports team—everyone doing what he or she thinks is best, and hoping it all fits together—usually means a really mean head coach is about to be hired.

Do sport teams empower individual team members to make decisions on their own? ("Instead of cutting to the left, as the play calls for, I think I'll cut to the right. I have a crazy hunch it will pay off.") No.

Do sports teams create an atmosphere where players are allowed—encouraged—to make mistakes? ("That was great, the way you roughed the kicker in there, Bruno, and got us a 20-yard penalty. Your learning curve is really up there.") No.

Do sports teams show the kind of loyalty and confidence to team members that they need to do good work? ("Sorry you hurt your ankle, Leroy. We're trading you to Cleveland.") No.

Sports teams are somewhat cross-functional. A team of 50 players will have many specialists. But the different functions seldom put their heads together. Offensive players may be friendly with defensive players—but they do not work together. And no one talks to the kicker.

The argument really breaks down over compensation and rewards. True teams are compensated at least partially on a team basis. One player helps another at the same position to succeed. Sports teams are dominated by superstars who take the lion's share of rewards, with journeymen and practice team members scrambling to pick up the scraps. Everyone is paid on individual contracts, according to individual rather than team performance. And good, loyal players are traded away the moment the team nears its salary cap.

Professional athletes know about only a narrow bandwidth of teamship. Just making the team is so competitive that a collaborative atmosphere afterward is hard to maintain. The first thing many athletes instruct their agents to negotiate is private rooms on the road. It used to be said of the Boston Red Sox, circa 1985, that after games they'd leave in 45 cabs.

Then there is the issue of gender and sensibility. Many men like pro sports, and some women like pro sports. But though pro sports are the coin of the realm to these fans, everyone else will be severely alienated by rah-rah gridiron exhortations.

Indeed, many women, dropped into this team environment, will wonder if they are expected to pick up a pair of pompoms and do splits.

Most of all, work teams do not work under the time constraints of pro sport teams. If we fail, we generally live to strive the next day. Pro sports is an unreal world of win/lose and sudden death elimination. Thank God we are not there—yet.

So what we say about sports metaphors is similar to what we said about adventure learning: it's great, and it's fun, but it is no substitute for the hard work of norming and storming that every team must pass through.

chapter 2 2

The Myth of Personality Type

e can encapsulate this chapter by saying that everything we said about adventure learning and teambuilding also holds true for the Myers-Briggs Type Inventory.

Adventure learning used mountaineering and other outdoor experiences to provide team members with new understandings about themselves. The Myers-Briggs personality categories also provide every team member with exhilarating new insights into themselves, and a set of initials (e.g., ENTP, ISTJ) that explain what kind of person they are. The Myers-Briggs instrument is more than a piece of paper to enthusiasts—it becomes the organizing principle of their lives.

Typology is based on the insight that there are many "archetypes" of people, that those types can be tested and defined, and that knowing what type we are relates directly to such down-to-earth business problems as leadership development, career decisions, and just plain getting along with others.

Founded on the insights of pioneer psychoanalyst C.G. Jung, typology holds that people can be divided into two perceiving or input groups (sensors and intuitors) and two judging or processing/output groups (thinkers and feelers). It measures the state of your current nature/nurture stew. Knowing where one falls on the continuum between the extremes can help you in making career moves, in delegating tasks you think are beyond you, in hiring and assigning people, and in working to strengthen your lesser talents.

I/E Introvert/Extrovert	S/N Sensing/Intuiting
T/F Thinking/Feeling	P/J Perceiving/Judging

People are different, Jung says, in the different ways they encounter the world. Broadly speaking, we either intuit or sense as we perceive and learn about the world. Intuitive types grasp the truth of a situation in a flash. They are the mysterious beings who never took notes in class, who guess for success . . . futuristic and imaginative. Sensing types, conversely, grope toward understanding in a step-by-step concrete way . . . here and now.

In addition to these two perception categories, we are also either one of two deciding categories. Quick judges of a situation are called feelers—emotion is their strong suit. Slow judgers are called thinkers—their strong suits are logic and method.

Overlaying these personality traits are the categories of Introverts and Extroverts. Where you are on this continuum leads to assumptions about which of the characteristics above you are prone to reveal to others.

The kind of perception you naturally prefer, either sensing or intuition, tends to team up with the kind of judgment you naturally prefer, whether thinking or feeling. The total result is a set of sixteen separate personality types combining the strengths of the eight possible Myers-Briggs categories.

All of us, according to the theory, have two strong sides and two recessive sides. In fact, type psychology breaks us down into dozens of additional characteristics, with lots of hyphens and brackets, superior characteristics and phantom or inferior ones—striving desperately to make us stereotypes even in our complexity.

Why do we include typology among our team myths? Because, just like adventure learning, typology has virtually nothing to do with teams.

It is not that personalities are unimportant. In our chapter on behavior differences, we stated that personalities are very different—and when they clash on the job, in the team, it's bad news.

But the Myers-Briggs Type Inventory does not measure anything that matters to teams. Teams do not rise or fall on how people are (either real or perceived) deep down inside. They rise or fall on what they actually do, how they actually behave toward one another on the outside.

Behavior, *sí*; typology, *no*.

The false assumption the Myers-Briggs makes is that personality reliably and consistently reveals itself in outside behaviors. It just ain't so. There are too many confounding life experiences that modify what we are into how we behave. Also, there are many segments of our population that delude themselves in terms of how they are viewed by others. They say to themselves, "Oh, I'm an introvert!" Maybe they drive through the neighborhood, shouting "I'm an introvert!" into a bullhorn. But they're wrong (Introverts don't do that).

All teams care about is what you *do*, in real terms, as seen through the eyes of other teammates. What you are inside is your business.

A wise man once said it this way: If one person calls you a horse's ass, well, it's just one person. If two people call you a horse's ass, well, there may be a conspiracy to label you a horse's ass. But if three people call you a horse's ass, you'd better invest in a saddle.

You can better determine what kind of a horse you are by getting behavioral feedback from team members than by filling out the MBTI questionnaire.

Tip: if you're really hell-bent on going the internally oriented (how you see yourself) Myers-Briggs route, don't use it in isolation. Combine it with an externally oriented (what you look like to others) inventory, like the Social Style Inventory from TRACOM of Denver, or the Personal Profile, DiSC, from Carlson Learning in Minneapolis. It's fascinating how our own image of ourselves can vary from the way others see us—and very relevant to team communication.

c h a p t e r   2 3

Myths of Team Leadership

eadership is the vessel for many of the worst team myths, for a logical reason. As keepers of the team vision, leaders make up a lot of stuff. Here are some of the worst illusions foisted on us by leaders about leadership.

▶ *Teams require a single individual to lead them.* It isn't so. There are many models of team leadership, ranging from traditional iron-hand rule through various degrees of self-direction to apparent leaderlessness. Leadership can rotate by the clock, or by the task at hand.

▶ *Strong leadership ensures success.* Again, it isn't so. Strong leadership is useless if the people following the leader are incompetent or uninterested in the team task. A fundamentally bad team cannot be "led"—except perhaps to a place of execution.

▶ *How a leader is selected is not important.* Wrong. Leaders must be selected in a way that is consonant with the task a team is assigned, and the kind of team he or she is assigned to. A free-wheeling, autonomous team will not welcome a leader assigned from outside the group. A new leader may have trouble adjusting to an established team. A team never previously allowed to make decisions for itself may be unable to choose its own leaders.

▶ *Team success is all that matters.* In a narrow sense, sure, team success matters to the team. But team success, whether driven by a strong leader or not, is meaningless if the task was wrong or duplicative or wasteful or pointless.

▶ *Team structure is a secondary consideration.* It isn't. Every team structure and configuration we are aware of—functionally aligned, cross-functionally aligned, matrix, network, single-leader, multiple-leader, leaderless—is valid, when applied to the appropriate team task. Perfect leadership and perfect follower-ship combined will still come to nothing unless the team is the right type of team for the task at hand.

▶ *A good leader and a good team can solve any task.* Sorry—not every task is appropriate for team action. If a task shouldn't be done by a team at all, it hardly matters who or how skilled its leader is. It's easy to get carried away with team fervor, but it's like the old saying, "When your only tool is a hammer, every problem looks like a nail."

The Myth of Senior Teams

Finally, there is the seriously mistaken notion that senior teams function like other teams, just in a more senior way. That teams at the top—teams comprised of board members, CEOs, presidents, vice presidents and other senior level execs—roll up their sleeves and collaborate in the same way that grunt teams do. They don't.

Anyone who has been on a senior team knows how rare true camaraderie is. The senior team table more closely resembles a play from the Renaissance, with dukes and earls and grand viziers jock-eying for advantage, than the kind of team we have been talking about. At the top levels, politics reigns supreme, and "team members" are there less to cooperate on joint action than to pursue constituent agendas.

This is partly because of the personality type that tends to rise to the top of organizations—Drivers with a bullet. Hard-charging executives prefer disposing to proposing, and they are typically rewarded for superior top-down, command-and-control performance. Except perhaps for the Vatican, large organizations do not turn to pastoral types for leadership.

But let's imagine that a generation of powerful, collaborative-minded managers rose suddenly to the top—people who share information, swap skill sets, and set their egos aside to achieve common objectives. In fact, this will happen someday, and not far in the future. Generation Xers and Yers are much more prone to team action than their Baby Boomer predecessors.

However, today's corporations will not welcome these generations, and will throw up powerful resistance to them. Today's organizations are modeled after patriarchal organizations established centuries ago, when leadership was envisioned in a singular, Driver-driven, masculine, competitive, Machiavellian way. Intrigue and manipulation are built into the charters of these organizations. To expect companies like IBM or Daimler-Chrysler or Harvard University to lead the way in describing a new kind of leadership by team, is to ask these organizations to go against their own natures.

Senior teams are "teams" in name only. They don't act like real teams because they are really parallel teams of one, each with their own constituents. Real teams share roles and responsibilities, whereas senior teams typically have parallel accountabilities. They are never able to prioritize goals since each member feels that his niche's goals are the most deserving.

Oh, it is sad and hypocritical. While top management encourages teamwork among the rank and file, they have no clue about it themselves. They can't. They are constitutionally prohibited from engaging in it. When top management cannot practice what it preaches, why should the rest of us take the preaching seriously?

Never, ever, look to top management for team leadership.

(Well, perhaps *never* is too strong. We will with the passage of time see the development of true senior teams. But it will happen in smaller, younger organizations. And it will be lifetimes before the model takes hold in their Fortune 500 counterparts.)

c h a p t e r   2 4

The Myth that People
Like Working Together

Say you have just been to a galvanizing seminar on teams, or read one of the excellent happy team books that abound on business bookshelves. You are excited about the potential teams have. You decide to "go team" with your colleagues.

You think, if we are to be a team, we must live, eat, breathe, and perform daily ablutions *as a team*. You tear down the cubicle walls, throw everyone in a pit together, sit back, and wait for those inevitable high-performance team results.

And wait. And wait.

You can wait till the cows come home, and high performance does not. The reason is that—surprise—people do not like being thrown into pits en masse.

We began this book with the wistful observation that most people have a real need, deep down, to work together. This is true in the aggregate. But we don't generally like being shackled to one another at the ankle. That's not a team, it's a chain gang.

People—average Americans, anyway—need their space to feel calm and safe. Spending the whole day in a playpen with teammates sounds less like a prescription for performance than a French drama of existential ennui.

Some of the most successful team environments we have visited don't feel all that "teamy" at first glance. In one highly successful team-oriented engineering company, the offices of team members are small, dimly lit, quiet, and include two desks facing away from one another. The engineers using the room are in constant contact, sharing information—but not smelling one another's breath. The overwhelming impression is of seclusion, not Monkey Island.

In designing a team environment, do not expect people to crave constant contact with one another. Honor their reluctance to lose their individual identity to the team.

It's a fine line you have to walk. People must be able to access one another instantaneously. There must be no communications snags anywhere. But people need their privacy, too.

Be aware that environment matters. Find out what works. Chances are it will be about midway between the penthouse and the outhouse.

chapter 25

The Myth that Teamwork Is More Productive than Individual Work

eams are great. Cuisinarts are also great. But you wouldn't mow your lawn with one.

The great sin of the age of teaming is that people are so high on the idea of teaming that they are asking teams to do everything. A job done by a team is better than a job done by a single individual. You get that synergy going, you know, all that shared information . . . yeah . . .

The truth is that teams are inherently inferior to individuals, in terms of efficiency. If a single person has sufficient information to complete a task, he or she will run rings around a team assigned the same task. There are no handoffs to other individuals. No misunderstandings or conflicting cultures. No colliding personalities, unless the individual is a multiple personality (see "Sybil Reengineering").

Beware. Teaming can be bad. Sometimes managers prefer teaming because it spreads accountability around, making blaming more difficult. Sometimes it means a bigger travel and entertainment budget. Or it means hand-picking team members.

The saddest thing we hear is "We were told we had to do everything as a team." The CEO is all ga-ga about teams, so now unless you do something as a team you're a pariah in your organization.

What's sad is that we hear it a lot. Mandatory teaming is misapplied team enthusiasm. It is anencephalic teaming. It is team tyranny, and people resent it.

chapter 2 6

The Myth of "The More, the Merrier" on Teams

ome people think that the larger the team, the better
the team.

Wrong.

* * *

OK, we'll elaborate a bit (although, a two-sentence chapter on
knowing when to stop seems very Zen or something).

There is a tendency by some executives to think of their entire
organization as a team. This is an interesting expression, but not a
useful one. Teams by their very nature can't be big. At some point
before a team exceeds the number of fingers on two hands, they
stop being teams and become mobs.

Team size is important. Smaller is much better than large. A team
can be self-led, leader-led, formal or ad-hoc, but it can't be humongous.

A strategic business unit is usually not a team. SBUs can range
from a score of people to several hundred, and they will be cross-
functional as all get-out, and they will talk about themselves as a
team—"We've got the Eastman Kodak Unit A Injection Molding
and Extrusion Team Spirit!" What they are is a network of teams.

Harvey was once called in to talk to an SBU. When he entered
the room, he saw 74 people sitting in chairs, about eight rows deep.
Harvey exhaled.

"OK," he said, "who here is on the team?" All 74 hands went up.

"Uh huh. If something goes wrong, how many people here get into trouble?" This time only about seven hands went up.

"OK. You people are the team. The rest of you are adjuncts. Go home."

For his part, Mike was ghosting a book about the Malcolm Baldrige National Quality Award, and had the opportunity to tour IBM Rochester, which had been touted as winning a giant proportion of points in its Baldrige scoring for its team orientation. The plant head had been quoted as saying that there were over 10,000 teams at the modest facility out on the Minnesota prairie.

So Mike drove to Rochester figuring he would walk down a lot of halls with rooms full of meeting teams. A city of teams. But after three hours of snooping around, he didn't see a single "team." The IBM Rochester definition of team was about as rigid as an amoeba. Whenever two people put their heads together on an ongoing basis, for a week or for a year, officially or unofficially, lean, mean, and transitory—that's a team.

Teams may sometimes seem larger than they are because of the adjuncts and resource personnel. These include:

▶ *core members*—the actual team, each one 100 percent dedicated to the team task

▶ *resource team member*—like the darting seagull, it drops its load and departs

▶ *support people*—people that help the core team get stuff done

▶ *team sponsor*—a manager the team can run to when it needs protection or direction

▶ *team champion*—the person who created the team

▶ *facilitators*—outside people who help keep the team on track

This is not to say that an SBU or a department or division or even an entire company can't cultivate "team spirit." Heck, even a multinational corporation can call itself a team if it wants to. It's a pleasant conceit, that sprawling, galactic, General Motors is simply "Team GM."

But . . .

c h a p t e r   2 7

The Myth that a Team Must Somehow Have More than One Team Member to Be a Team

I f teams mustn't be too big, how small can they be before they stop being teams?

We define a team as being two persons or more. But it may be useful, as you sort through the people available to you, to consider "the team of one."

People think we're joking when we talk about teams of one ("Why would you call a person a team?") but we're not.

A team of one is a virtual team, a single person with lots of diverse expertise treated by others as a separate team.

In complex organizations, it's very common for teams to interact. A new product team, for instance, will have dealings with the design team down the hall. They'll get input from another team in finance, and another team in marketing. Usually these teams have a number of people on them. Occasionally, though, the connection is a single person. When this happens, it is good team politics to treat that person just like a bona fide team. You extend him or her the courtesy you would extend a group. Just because the team is a singleton does not allow you to go on a blaming rampage.

Meanwhile, contemplate the beauty of the team of one. It means that instead of putting several people from different functions on the team, the team's diversity is integrated in a single person. Think of the arguments that never happen. Think of the handoffs that never take place. Think of the rapidity with which the team gets through the storming phase.

Diversity of knowledge is the reason for teams. But the age of the corporate specialist is yielding to the age of the one-man-band—technology driven, entrepreneurial jacks of all trades.

A team of one is so much faster, and so much more unambiguous than a team of more than one.

A team of one is also a splendid way to outplace a team member who doesn't work well on a close, daily basis with your team, but whose knowledge remains valuable—or someone who just doesn't want to belong to you. Simply take the individual out of the team box, draw a dotted line to a box that is all his own, and poof, you have a team of one serving as a resource to the team. No muss, no fuss, and everyone is happy.

chapter 2 8

The Myth that Teams Work Everywhere

The two of us traveled to São Paulo to give a talk about teams. We flew down, gave our usual "teams-are-great-but-problematic " talk, and we witnessed something that disturbed us. It was something exceedingly simple that became exceedingly complicated.

We went to the Brazilian equivalent of a convenience store to get a bottle of water. The man at the canteen counter asked what type we wanted and how much we wished to spend. We explained that we wanted mineral water in the half-liter plastic bottle. He told us the cost (1.40 Reales, about $1.50) and directed us to the cashier at the end of the counter, a woman who took our money and then hand-wrote a receipt for it. We took this receipt back to the counter and waited for the man to show up again, as the cashier called him back from the back room. In a moment a third person approached, with no knowledge of us or the deal we had struck a minute earlier. After we went through the choices again, he opened a cooler door, and there we saw, for the first time, water. We handed him the receipt, and he surrendered the water.

It was a remarkably inefficient process, one that cried out for reengineering. Probably the store needed a "team of one"—a single person to take the money and hand over the bottle. There wasn't enough work to justify the three people operating in functional silos.

But here's the problem. People are plentiful in São Paulo. They arrive every day by the thousands, without skills, drawn by the promise of jobs.

Since people power in Brazil is cheap (40 percent of the population makes less than $120 per month), downsizing hasn't occurred there yet, as it has in Argentina. So organizations remain very hierarchical, with lots of bosses, and lots of levels. Our purpose for being there was to talk about a nonhierarchical approach, the self-directed work teams that have taken over American and Japanese business.

Brazil, like much of the developing world, still has one foot planted firmly in the era of control, of dictators, bosses, and the military model. If you don't commit to the idea of trusting people and to the free flow of information throughout an organization, developing teams isn't just a wrong idea, it can be catastrophic.

But business people we spoke to were still very interested. Their economy is handicapped by high costs and low productivity, which hamper global competitiveness. This book, which has done modestly well in America, is a much bigger deal in Brazil. We couldn't walk by a newsstand without seeing it displayed. But by the end of our trip, because of the danger teams pose in controlling environments, we were tempted to hide the book behind other titles.

On the one hand, Brazil needs teams to achieve efficiencies, become more competitive, and generate more wealth for itself. But on the other hand, the process of becoming more efficient means downsizing that little convenience store, and a million operations like it. Just because teams and downsizing had a generally healthy (albeit painful) effect on the U.S., does not mean Brazil's pain—which will be catastrophically higher—would be justified.

What happens when, using computers to replace people, you downsize a society where a quarter of the people are already living in cardboard shacks on the outskirts of town, along the banks of the city's two lifeless rivers, without running water or electricity?

In America, the two of us are like ambulance drivers, helping teams that have been in car crashes. But abroad, where teams have not caught on, we're more like ambassadors for an idea that may do them more harm than good.

part four

Turning Teams Around

▼

chapter 29

Moving Teams through Stages
toward Success

ay back in the 1970s, psychologist B.W. Tuckman identified four stages of team development that he felt all teams had to pass through in order to be successful. They are:

▶ *Forming.* When a group is just learning to deal with one another; time in which minimal work gets accomplished.

▶ *Storming.* A time of stressful negotiation of the terms under which the team will work together; a trial by fire.

▶ *Norming.* A time in which roles are accepted, team feeling develops, and information is freely shared.

▶ *Performing.* When optimal levels are finally realized—in productivity, quality, decision making, allocation of resources, and interpersonal interdependence.

With or without tests or team-building sessions, all successful teams go through all four of these stages. Sometimes a team gets lucky, and its mix of personalities, or the kind of leadership that emerges among its members, brings the group from Forming to Performing with a minimum of struggle. But no team goes directly from Forming to Performing. Struggle and adaptation are critical, difficult, but very necessary parts of team development.

Identifying where your team is along the pathway toward success and how to move it from one stage to the next with minimum resistance are important factors distinguishing great teams from dysfunctional ones.

The Forming Stage

Forming is that stage in the development of a team when everything is up for grabs, and when a team is only a team in the loosest sense of the word. The talent may all be right there in front of you. Good engineers, good planners, good production people, good finance staff. But like a drill sergeant surveying his newest platoon on the first day of boot camp, you've never seen such a ragtag bunch of unsoldierly individuals in all your born days.

Did you ever, as a kid, transfer to a new school? Remember what that first day felt like? Walking to school you had one burning desire for the year, to do well, like Mom and Dad said. Once you took your place among all the other faces, however, all that changed. What mattered, instead, was being accepted by all these strangers. They were going to be important adjuncts in your life for the foreseeable future, and you wanted them to like you.

That overwhelming need to fit in, meanwhile, was met with a certain native opposition to adapting. No one wants to run up the white flag, unconditionally surrendering his or her personal identity—we all want to remain ourselves even while we fit into the group. We want "more information" on what we've gotten ourselves into. We want to know who's in charge, and what they're likely to require of us.

It's exactly the same with teams. We ache to plunge in, but first we need to know how cold the water is. That is the ambivalent mindset we bring to joining new teams. One of the signs of a team at the Forming stage is an overweening politeness, a bending over backwards to be pleasant, not to offend, not to ruffle feathers.

Everyone has his 15 seconds of self-introduction, then sits down, eyes darting nervously. This is understandable when you consider that manners are generally instituted to keep strangers from frightening one another; the hand extended in friendship supposedly is an ancient way of demonstrating that one is bringing peaceful intentions to the relationship, not a blackjack.

This eagerness to appear nonthreatening is really a key to how threatening Forming usually is: people getting together for the first time with all sorts of questions about which members have power and whether they will share it, and with whom, doubts about one's own abilities and the abilities of others, and prejudices about the types of people one is likely to be paired off with.

Amid these unsettling feelings, people cast about anxiously for something—anything—to form temporary alliances around. It can be something as simple as two people smoking the same brand of cigarettes, a preference for the same vein of humor, or being about the same height, or having worked with competing businesses in the past. Anything that pairs or triads can use to derive feelings of safety from the larger group. (*Forming* is the birthplace of the clique.)

During the Forming stage, potential teammates identify similarities and expectations of outcomes, agree on the team's purpose, and identify possible resources and skill sets. They get to know each other and begin to bond, evaluate trust levels and, as much as possible, communicate personal needs.

The challenge of Forming is the challenge of giving an inert group of people who don't know each other a collective kickstart. Here are some of the questions to which a group in Forming, in order to get going with a minimum of pain, must find answers:

▶ Why was I asked to participate on this team?

▶ Whose idea was the formation of this team?

▶ Why were we formed?

▶ Who are the other members, and what are their strengths?

▶ How am I going to find out what they're good at, and also let them know of my capabilities and characteristics?

▶ How large should the team be in order to accomplish the team goal quickly?

▶ Should team membership be voluntary or mandatory?

▶ How and when are we going to bring needed resources onto the team, and get rid of them when they're no longer needed?

People who are new to one another cast about desperately for subject matter. All too typically they alight on the organization itself, and establish some signal with one another that it is OK to poke fun at the company. Within moments of being put together they can be hard at work fashioning a caricature of the company they work for—so like the drawings of "Teacher" that got them in trouble in the fourth grade, and still a way to achieve an easy, preliminary consensus twenty or forty years later. Someone or something must pay the price, serving as a safety valve for the tension in a group just getting together.

Forming is a time of great danger. First impressions are made, and then set in concrete. Aggressive personalities move quickly to establish dominance. Alliances are formed, and counter-alliances. Signals are flashed back and forth, mysterious even to the transmitters. While the mass of group members silently mouth the words, *Why are we here?*, a few individuals may try to provide their own answers.

Besides team size and configuration, other issues must be resolved early on. Who "owns" the team? Does management own you, or do you own yourselves? By ownership, we mean commitment. Typically a new group has a weak focus on its sense of purpose, and therefore has a hard time feeling very proprietary about what it's doing. In Forming, ownership is virtually all management's. But before a team comes full circle, it will reverse those proportions and will feel a bond of commitment so strong it will have at least a few insecure people in top management scratching their heads. The team must belong not to management, nor to the groups each team member (on cross-functional teams) represents. It must eventually belong to the team itself.

The biggest monkey wrench a team member can throw into a problem-solving session is the statement, "I'll take that back to the division and see what my people will say." Yes, that's how the rest of the world works. It "sounds" good; it sounds responsible and politic. It buys time. It spares members the pain of saying "no" today. But it's not how effective teams operate. Members of effective teams come to the table already empowered; they wouldn't be on the team if they didn't have the authority to make judgments for their groups on their own. If a team member insists on taking every decision back to "the membership," it's probably time to push the button on his EJECT seat. Oh, and while you're at it, take this back to "your people." *Sproing.*

A final consideration: Who is a member and who is not? We have seen teams struggle with the drag weight of members who would rather be vacuuming the Mojave Desert than participating on the team. In some cases, it was because they were intransigent jerks. In many, many cases, however, it was not their fault—they truly were too busy, or they truly were convinced that another approach was better than the one the team was moving toward. But they were afraid to "drop out" lest they experience dire repercussions in their chosen career fields.

Management must be very, very honest—with the team and with itself—and it must say, in the most unmistakable terms possible, "No one will be punished if they decline to participate on this team. No recriminations and no ramifications, no loyalty oaths, no blacklists, no demotions. You have our permission to leave."

This is still not perfect. Few team members will walk away cheerfully, naive enough to think no one noticed them beating their hasty retreat, and no one will remember or retaliate for their departure. The work world will probably inflict pain on people who quit their teams. That's regrettable. But the team is better off without them.

One of the greatest dangers of all is that someone in the group, a quick study, will want to push forward too quickly, to vault over Storming and Norming, and to go directly into Performing. The quick study may feel there is no time to waste, and much progress to be achieved by sprinting to the finish line. But there are no short-cuts to team development. For now, the most important job for this team is not to build a better rocket or debug a beta version of a new software product or double sales—it is to orient itself to itself.

The Storming Stage

It is estimated that three-fifths of the length of any team project, from start to finish, is taken up with the first two stages, Forming and Storming. In German literature there is a style characterized as *sturm und drang,* "storm and stress," referring to an exaltation of individual sensibilities.

The same could be said to apply to Storming as the pathway to team building. Rank with individual emotion, group conflict, and change, Storming is not for the squeamish. The best that can be said for it is that it is necessary, and it gets things out of the way. What a team fails to settle during Storming will surely return to haunt it at a later date—and probably to return the team, kicking and screaming, to the eye of its own Storm.

There has never been a team that was not first tested in the Storming phase. And Storming always comes as a surprise, no matter how well one prepares for it. The best one can hope for is that it not drag on forever, as a gruesome war of attrition that no faction can win. To prevent that there are some guidelines teams still in formation may follow.

Leadership is of paramount importance. If you are the "leader" of a new team and you leave them all alone to sort out their conflicts, writing them a blank check to take as long as the sorting-out takes, shame on you.

Now is the time to be stepping in, explaining limits, offering suggestions, keeping a lid on the inevitable anarchy. You do not want

Storming to outgrow the office, spill over into the lunchroom, run riot in the streets, and finally head down the road, torches ablaze, pitchforks poised, toward the Bastille. You're not ready for that yet.

During Forming the leader's role was essentially directive—to point out where people were headed until the group could configure its own bearings. During Storming the leader continues to direct traffic, but now taking on the additional role of the coach—the person who not only tells you what to do, but helps with suggestions on how to get there.

Coaching is critical because Storming is where the most important dimensions of a team are worked out—its goals, its roles, its relationships, identifying likely barriers, and the infrastructure support mechanisms necessary to sustain long-term team health. Together with its goals, which the team began establishing during Forming, clarifying and implementing these four elements comprise the entire agenda of teaming.

The coach is there to help, but not to interfere. It is a delicate tightrope-walking act that he or she has to put on, because morale may dip to new lows, and hostilities will emerge and demand some kind of reaction. One rule we emphasize is that you can say just about anything, but that personal destructiveness will be frowned upon, and probably squashed like a bug. Sniping, blaming, and belittling remarks that have no bearing on the work of the team are pure poison—to the targeted individual, but also to the sense of trust necessary for the team to function as a whole.

When you first see signs of personal poison bubbling to the surface, that's when it's time to call time out. People have work to do—tormenting one another is not merely wrong, it's irrelevant to the team's mission.

As with Forming, there are questions during Storming that need answering in order for the group to make progress. They include:

▶ What are we supposed to accomplish as a team?

▶ What are each of our roles and responsibilities, as they relate to accomplishing the goal?

▶ Who do each of us need to get information from, and to whom does our information have to go in order to complete our goal? Where are our linkages to the outside world?

▶ If we get into trouble, who can we get to rescue us? Who will accept the responsibility of sponsoring this group and its activities?

▶ Who's in charge? Will that change from day to day, from one phase of the project to the next? How do we adapt to changing leadership?

▶ How will we arrive at decisions? When will we know we have done that?

▶ What happens when we fight? How do we resolve disagreements over goals or procedures?

▶ How do we increase our ability to take risks until we get to the most direct, most creative level?

▶ What strengths do each of us bring to bear on accomplishing our goal? How can we focus our strengths to influence activities outside our own team?

▶ When will we meet, and how (large groups, small groups, one-on-one, etc.)?

▶ How are we going to make ourselves more accessible to one another in order to complete our goals in a timely manner?

▶ Where (or who) are the team's supports? Where (or who) are our detractors and stumbling blocks?

A team that manages to answer these questions in the early stages of Storming will minimize the pain of a necessarily painful process. Remember that Storming takes as much time as there are issues in need of resolution. It is not a difficult task for teams made up of like-minded individuals—all design engineers, say. Cross-functional teams are by nature made up of primarily unlike-minded individuals.

Ask and answer these questions on a regular basis, and you can change the name of the stage from *storming* to *clarifying*. The storm is no longer an unpredictable, destructive thunderhead front that approaches, drops rain, and blows itself out. It's more like an irrigation system that you can turn on and off at will, challenging the team on a regular, structured basis to root out the differences of opinion that lurk, unspoken.

Leaders will want to run periodic checks on their own status. Are they still the leader, or has a coup already occurred, without bloodshed? Often leaders are deposed, usually without animosity. If you are deposed on the grounds that someone else within the team is a more natural internal leader, chill. Chances are management knew this would happen all along, and that your job, which was to get the group cranked up, has been accomplished. You may continue as a conduit of information to higher management. You may find you truly have become unnecessary, a sixth finger, and you may wish to move on to new challenges, or just go fishing.

In any event, these things happen during Storming. The only wrong reaction in such a circumstance is to get all defensive. No insult was intended. The group you helped form has made its first decision.

Leaders should understand the signs of Storming. Storming is hope mingled with a large dose of fear. During Storming, every team member is wondering if he is respected by the others. Some members will be hostile or overzealous. Some will be intimidated. Pulses will race. Sleep will be lost. Jealousy and infighting, competition and polarization are the orders of the day. Alliances which seemed solid one day come crashing apart the next. Some individuals will rush too soon into the cauldron and offer to be boiled down into "team." Others will resist membership, the compromise of their individuality, their standoffishness, as if their lives depended on it.

The worst news of all for leaders is that Storming extracts a high toll from them personally. Among the many charming occurrences in mid-storm is a rash of blaming that generally trashes leadership at all levels. Suddenly, you're the reason the group can't coalesce, you're the reason deadlines aren't met, you're the reason individuals feel unfulfilled, misunderstood, deadended. As team members wrestle with their identity and direction, leaders are led out for judgment, sometimes gagged and bound.

We have seen leaders go white-knuckled with rage at the accusations teams needed to trump up as part of their "rite of passage." You weren't there when we needed you, is a common refrain. You only cared about yourself, they say, to an individual who may have lost sleep every night for a year because they couldn't get their act together, while the leader grappled with deciding how to intervene, and whether to intervene.

It can be hilarious to watch, when a leader who has been patronizing his team is suddenly made aware of that fact (hilarious so long as you're not the leader, anyway). More often, though, it is just a painful ordeal. Like all developmental stages, there is no alternative to riding out the storm. If it is any comfort, we offer to leaders the solace that what at first sight appeared to be a "personality conflict" is really nothing of the sort. And that may be the saving beauty of Storming—it truly is about team formation, and only superficially about personalities.

One of the most challenging events in the life of a team is the introduction of new members. Say that your team got through the Storming phase, and it took six months from your company's lifeblood. The very last thing you want to see happening with that project is a return to those halcyon days of yore. But that's what often happens when someone new is thrown in with an established team. That person will say things like, "But that isn't how we did it at Hyperion," and "We need to talk about some of these procedures from the ground up."

It's human nature to want new team members to feel welcome, and for them to be quickly and cleanly folded in with the rest of the group. But their earnest suggestions that the game return to GO and start over again may have to be resisted, or redirected. The very best thing to do with new team members is to take them aside, for a week if necessary, and bring them up to speed on the history of the team, the decisions it has made and committed itself to, and the reasons why it is perilous to drag them all back to Square One in order to help orient a single new member.

Some people will object that it is too expensive to train new people so exhaustively, to answer all their questions, that they won't be able to absorb all the new information in one fell swoop. The answer is that it is far more expensive to leave the newcomer with a head full of questions, and the potential any loose cannon has to blow a hole through the deck.

Another option is what we call the "modified limited backslide," in which you permit the group to reenter the Storming phase, in order to orient new individuals or rehash an unsolved problem, but with the strong proviso that Storming be brought to a clear conclusion by a preset deadline. You may have to swallow hard before you take this step, but sometimes, when the group shows signs it needs to reevaluate its direction, it is imperative. If you do not signal a retreat, the troops will bug out on their own.

Storming is the stage at which a few people will decide to stonewall. They still show up for work, and they may still communicate with other team members, after a fashion. But if you look closely at their behaviors, it becomes clear that the team at hand is not the team they wanted, so they have decided against being enthusiastic members.

Sometimes an entire team graduates from Storming except for one individual, yet the team finds itself unable to go on to the next stage—the holdout has them all by the shirttails, keeping them in place, while he storms on. For an individual like this, there are only two sensible options—to get with the team, or get out. At the same time, the team and the company owe the problem person a second chance, maybe even a third chance, to reconsider his or her standoffishness and rejoin the team.

Perhaps the worst consequence of Storming is that production may be at a standstill for weeks, even months at a time. For management, that is the bottom line of Storming—wasted time and blown projects. Somehow this chaotic process must be kept from mutating into ongoing turmoil.

To the extent that we can say that the process of teamwork works, it is in the minimizing of this necessary but painful period in the life of a group. The best analogy we have yet heard for Storming is that it is like internal combustion. If you place a teaspoon of gasoline on a sidewalk it quickly disperses, more or less harmlessly. Compressed in an engine cylinder, however, its vaporized particles begin to bounce into one another at supersonic speeds. Ideally, a controlled explosion occurs, and a vehicle many thousands of times the weight and size of that teaspoon of fuel begins to move.

When that happens, the storm has broken. Roles clarify. A team style begins to materialize. The sun returns to the sky, and a calmer, new day dawns for everyone.

The Norming Stage

With the passing of the storm comes a new alignment and acceptance of roles within the team. The success experienced during the Norming stage is a success marked by contradiction—the group becomes stronger as individuals let down key defenses, acknowledge weaknesses, and ask for help from people with compensating strengths.

The Norming stage is defined by acceptance of the very roles that Storming raged against. Relationships that began in the Forming stage as superficial events—coincidences of cigarette brands, favorite jokes, and alma maters—have the opportunity to deepen during Norming.

What's more, the group can finally be said to have a relationship with itself. It can show affection for individual members in the form of banter and repartee (often a male response), and genuine consideration. During Norming the ragged edges of conflict begin to subside. Tension ebbs, and many individuals now poke their heads out, like forest creatures after a summer downpour, to realize it is OK to come out of hiding.

What has happened is that the hidden agendas covertly advanced by members during Storming ("I want to lead," "I want to be left alone," "I reserve the right to disagree on any subject at any time") have been unmasked, or have diminished in importance. People's needs to assert their dominion over the group, whether actively or passively, shrink in proportion to the growth of their intimate knowledge of the group.

As the group becomes less threatening, individual members mount fewer threats against it. Even individuals who are still conflicted tend to keep conflict from bubbling over and affecting other people's work. People take care not to derail or sabotage the hard-won feeling of teamhood the group now enjoys.

As group members become more docile, the group as a whole gains in focus and unanimity. A splendid dynamic of peeling away occurs, in which every dismantled individual defense is used to shore up the group instead. "Weaknesses" are reconstituted as strengths. Information is freely shared, and the group conducts periodic agenda checks to remind itself of its goals and take note of its progress.

During Forming leaders were crucial, to get the group going. During Storming leaders were the sacrificial victim, as struggling teams groped to achieve consensus at the leaders' expense. Now, during Norming, formal leadership begins to fade, as important data is no longer exclusive to leadership. In the next stage, Performing, leadership becomes a part of everyone's job, and mutual interdependence becomes the order of the day.

For the first time, the group may be pictured as a kind of great hulking beast, now able to move in a single direction, if haltingly, upon command. Before long, the great beast will be doing the merengue. For the first time, the group is a true team.

The Performing Stage

There is no guarantee that your team will make it as far as Performing. As Hamlet said in one of his reveries on team playing, "'Tis a consummation devoutly to be wished." The workforces of America are riddled with teams that never emerge from Storming, who continue to batter or ignore one another. They may call what they are doing every day from nine to five Performing, but the numbers are never there, and neither is the feeling.

Performing is not workaholism. In a way it's the opposite, because it is the admission by every member of the team that he or she cannot do the job alone. This is a level of genuine commitment to company goals and objectives that may be new to individual team members. A workaholic, by contrast, is someone who works every weekend. Workaholics think they're indispensable, and the rest of the world are morons.

Performers know the real worth of everyone they work with. Performing team members don't get all bent out of shape if they're called over the weekend to help solve a pressing problem. Performing means being sufficiently in touch with one's own needs and requirements that one can fashion a work schedule that assures progress in team projects, without twisting one's own priorities beyond recognition.

Performing is a time of great personal growth among team members. With the sharing of the experiences, feelings, and ideas of other team members comes a new level of consciousness—the sense of knowing where other team members are at, a sense of fierce loyalty even to members you may not be friendly with, and a willingness to find a way through nearly any challenge that arises.

Performing means that the team becomes "fly-eyed"—seeing with many eyes instead of just two. This means a reduction in blind spots. It means that the team, encountering an elephant blindfolded, will be able to identify it as exactly what it is—an elephant.

Performing means intimacy. With performing, members may move beyond the locker-room banter of playful teasing into a dimension of communicating that is less self-conscious and less afraid. The humor may linger on, but the little missiles we fire at one another throughout the workday may be disarmed. The humor will reflect a lesser degree of veiled aggression, and a greater degree of caring. Intimacy means understanding that a job is much more than "a job"—that one's pride, livelihood, and chances for happiness, security, and fulfillment are all riding on these balky contracts with our employers.

Intimacy means acknowledging the seriousness of individual team members' requirements, and pooling together to help ensure that every member succeeds, with the help of every other member. Conflict does not filter into the upper atmosphere during Performing. Indeed, it is more in evidence than ever. Perhaps it is because conflicts are put on the table, and not reshuffled into the deck, that Performing works so well. Disagreements are confronted, discussed, considered, and adjudicated.

What during Storming seemed destructive—people at odds over project and turf issues—seems during Performance to be healthy and positive. Once an argument is resolved, team members resume working together. "Losing" an argument doesn't mean you get roasted; "winning" doesn't mean you get to scorch the loser. The order of the day during Performing is, "a good, clean fight." The atmosphere is one of enthusiasm and *esprit de corps*.

Best of all, apart from all this progress in the feel-good dimension, the team is going great guns. Deadlines are being met, production is up to par, and the speed of information flow defies the usual mechanism of memo routing, weekly meetings, and quality checks. People are getting their work done properly, on time, and in coordinated sequence.

And the word goes out throughout the company, throughout the region: *Look out for the team over in* [your project name goes here]. *I think they're on to something.*

They're on to something, all right. It's called teamwork.

chapter 30

Teams and Technology

A dozen years ago team processes were slow but simple. People worked together, met together, spent Miller Time together—they virtually lived together, in one place. The team was likely all male, all white, and all of them—Bob, Tom, Al, and Dave—drove to the same bedroom community when the working day was done.

No more. A handful of mighty forces have broken up the old gang. Some companies have gone global, spreading teams across a score or more time zones and three or four continents. Telecommuting has undermined the sense of office solidarity. Corporate alliances with strategic partners mean that team members may not even be working for the same company.

The move toward workplace diversity has further stirred the stew. A team today is about as mixed up as a team could be. And the most obvious victim of this mix-up is the Monday morning meeting. Bob is still on the team, but he is joined by Christine, Dewayne, Abdul, and Xiaoping, plus a subteam in Sweden, plus auxiliary members at a dozen partner organizations, three of them in Singapore.

Instead of being all together in one place, the new team is scattered across the face of the globe. English is not the first language for the majority of team members. They come from different cultures, with different assumptions. They live in different time zones. They are paid in different money.

Go, team.

Technology is what made this kind of global teamwork possible. With luck, technology just might help it all work.

Grappling with Groupware

Few pieces of technobabble are as misunderstood as the word *groupware.*

Groupware is a kind of contradiction—personal software that is for groups. In the beginning, groupware products addressed two main problems, controlling workflow (process) and regulating work content (substance). But now, with the Internet and wireless communications, groupware functions are all over the place.

We describe four different classifications of groupware, according to when each is used, and where.

Same Time/Same Place

The conventional meeting—team members sitting together in a room and talking—is the ultimate and the archetypal Same Time/Same Place technology. For vividness, clarity, and social strokes, nothing will ever take its place.

But meetings have their own tyranny, wasting time and team energy. And people simply can't meet Wednesdays at 2 P.M. in the conference room like they used to. So conventional meetings are giving way, thanks to technology, to new ways of meeting, in different places and at different times.

One of the most interesting Same Time/Same Place applications is electronic voting systems, such as OptionFinder. OptionFinder is a handheld remote hooked up via wires or wireless to a PC. Team members use the remote to vote on issues that arise, and the software displays the votes immediately, prompting discussion on why the team differed. The conversation leads the team to the next level, beyond politeness to true inquiry.

We have seen teams that thought they were in perfect agreement, but weren't getting anything done, use a tool like OptionFinder to flush out their deeper opinions. Suddenly they have to confront resistance, disparagement, dismissiveness, or genuinely good reasons why they disagree.

Same Time/Different Place

This is technology that allows people to communicate simultaneously across distance—but not across so much that one party is likely to be asleep while the other is awake. It was the miracle of the ages once—the telegraph, the telephone, ham radio. Before that, we relied on smoke signals and drums. More recent developments include two-way video, screen sharing, live online chat boards, teleconferencing, and fax on demand.

Different Time/Same Place

Think of the 100-year teams that built the cathedrals in Rouen and Chartres—multiple-lifetime projects occurring on a single site.

These are programs that team members can plug into on-site, at a time of their choosing—any multiple-input, round-the-clock system. A Post-It note tabbed to the chair of the worker sitting at your desk during the shift after yours. The office itself, with all its books, tools, and support systems, is a "technology" meeting this definition.

One of the first electronic steps away from Same Time/Same Place team action was also one of the most significant—single-site networking, such as at a plant where three shifts of workers must somehow be in constant communication, around the clock. That solution, first implemented back in the 1960s, was the beginning of e-mail.

Different Time/Different Place

E-mail and networking quickly moved beyond a single site. In so doing it paved the way for the development of workgroup computing systems like Lotus Notes, a powerful messaging, planning, and organizing tool. Notes is the avatar of a whole new era of groupware products that will link networked teams together across time and space. But Notes, while flexible and easy to use, still represents the tip of the iceberg of the new meeting technologies.

Other examples include voicemail, online services like America Online and Microsoft Network, Internet gateways, and fax.

This is the most-publicized groupware grouping, and it will only become more dominant as the Web continues to grow worldwide.

Does Technology Work?

Deciding what technology is best for your team is a big question, involving everything currently on the market, and intuiting what is about to occur and what the next standards will be.

We can't go through all that. But we can ask some diagnostic questions about the technology you currently have in place, and whether it is helping the team be a team or keeping it from being one.

The Internet is the greatest team tool the world has ever seen. It allows people spread far apart to be sharing information 24 hours a day. It frees individuals from numerous rote tasks and allows them to use parts of the brain higher up the stem. Some perfect combination of phones, faxes, computers, modems, and group software products can lift your team to remarkable levels of achievement. But chances are, you've got the wrong combination in place.

Does Your Team Run Your Computer System, or Does the Computer System Run Your Team?

You want your people to be functioning like adults, not reduced to tears by some idiot batch command loop that they can't get out of. A great system is one which people can log onto, access what they need, and change what needs changing, without having to call in the system administrator. As your processes evolve, your system should be able to evolve with it. Problem is, most networks are still much too hard to use.

Is the Team Really More Productive, or Do They Just Look Busy?

This is the biggie. Labor statistics say that office automation is leading an upsurge in productivity in every country in the world. Downsizing, the shucking off of unneeded personnel, and teaming, the elimination of the supervisory level, are offshoots of this surge. But not every activity belongs on-screen. Lots of activities still work better the old way—paper calendars, yellow legal pads, and No. 2 pencils.

Are Security Concerns Undoing the Benefits of Your Network?

Teams thrive on trust. Your Intranet is supposed to keep people in constant touch with one another, via e-mail, shared data, and computer conferencing. Too many levels of passwords, too many firewalls, or too obsessive an attitude about data security, can effectively lock people away from one another—putting your budding team right back on square one.

Are Teams Properly Trained, or Are They Put Out There to Sink or Swim?

Most team members need training, and not just on-the-job. Microsoft Excel, Lotus Notes, and the Internet are not intuitive ideas, no matter what your tech consultant told you. Bad training begets inefficiency and error. Some organizations have been successful by having workers who are already expert at key programs and technologies take the lead in training the incoming.

Are Team Suggestions Welcome, Invited, Rewarded?

It's to an organization's advantage to make team members lightning rods for process improvements, including technological processes. If team members come up with tips on how to use the software more efficiently, or how to move data from place to place with fewer problems, solicit them, and spread the word.

Are Technological Innovations Messing People Up?

You can have too much of a good thing. Many teams have exulted in their new Intranet, or voicemail setup, only to be capsized by the torrent of messages. New Internet subscribers often complain about logging in to perform a task, but first having to wade through 100 e-mail messages.

Technology can also undercut team feeling. Computers are a great help for teams scattered across a wide area, but they can put a real dent in teams occupying the same quarters. E-mail is great, but nothing beats good old face-to-face conversation. There is no such thing (yet) as a virtual water cooler, or a digital bull session.

Has Freedom Led to Chaos?

A team member turns telecommuter, and now works from home. To some extent he now manages himself, but not completely. How do you keep people you never break bread with connected and in touch with team goals? Has your company devised a plan to keep all its lone rangers from galloping off in a dozen different directions?

And how does a team leader practice MBWA—"managing by walking around"—when "around" is so far around?

What used to be a team of people working 9 to 5 in the same shoebox is now a bewildering array of all kinds of people working all sorts of crazy hours, reporting in a variety of different ways. Workers in such conditions require more attention, not less.

Is Your Technology a Substitute for Real Change?

The blessing of the Internet and Intranets is that they can cut employees loose from order-giving, double-checking, top-down hierarchies: "Do this and don't ask questions." But they work all right with old-style preteam structures, too. "Computer sweat-shop" is not an oxymoron. Don't assume, just because your team is wired and online, that they understand it's OK now to think. Let your computers be clones, and your people be people.

Technology and Personality

Sometimes teams imagine that all they have to do is select an appropriate technology, master it as a team, and go forward. They forget that the team exists, that it is better than disconnected individuals, because the differentness of its members deepens and enriches performance.

We are not just different in and of ourselves. We are also different in the ways we approach and engage with technology.

Sometimes the differentness resolves itself neatly. Imagine there are only two "tech personalities"—Power Users, who eat, drink, and breathe technology, and Pluggers, who get it, but only eventually.

If a team is made of three Power Users and five Pluggers, the Power Users teach the Pluggers how to use the software or hardware, and all is well. The teaching actually aids in team formation—it cements a bond.

There are, however, more than just those two personality types.

Yes, there are *Power Users*—the early adapters, the people technology is rolled out to first. They learn it, and become teachers.

Pluggers are the earnest students who pick up the lessons as quickly as they can. They are no great shakes at using systems, but they give as good as they get, and don't complain.

The rest of the team could be all over the place.

Some are *People Persons*. They think in terms of feelings and organic relationships. Systematic thinking of the sort you need to learn file transfer protocols isn't in their natures.

Those with *Artistic Dispositions* never quite get with the program. They are self-directed, and can't be bothered with the universe the software wants to superimpose over our own. They use computers and software in a halting, unenthusiastic fashion.

Some are *Worriers* by nature. Their fear that something will go wrong prevents them from ever exploring the way a complex system like the Internet or Windows Registry needs to be explored. But they keep great backups.

Some people are *Overenthusiasts*. They get so immersed in the trivia of technology that they lose sight of the big scheme. They decline to read manuals and help files, but cheerfully badmouth the company in Usenet forums. They buy too impulsively, with too little research, and too late at night.

Others of are of the *Executive* temperament, whether they rule from the penthouse or mop up the outhouse. They aren't patient with steep learning curves. Dole it out for them up front or get out of our sight. The worst people with technology are corporate (non-IT) bosses.

And you have your bona fide *Technophobe,* rare but still out there and bemoaning the existence of anything more advanced than a one-horse dray. To the true Technophobe, anything electronic is the spawn of Satan, and all its promises are cruel lies. (He's right, but does he have to be so cocksure about it?)

There are dozens more types. *Dabblers, One-Note Johnnies, Sloths, Misers, Whiners*—you know them. The point is that we are all different, but we are all sold the same systems with the same materials, aimed at only one or two types, the Power User and the Plugger. The rest of us are left to scratch our heads and wonder what it's like to be part of progress.

What this means is that not only must a team battle itself to express and appreciate one another's ideas, but it must battle the different levels of enthusiasm with which team members use the tools of communication.

Have you ever sent a teammate a time-bound message by e-mail, assuming she, like you, checks her e-mail box every day? Maybe that message was important. Is she to blame because she doesn't like e-mail? Or are you to blame for not knowing she doesn't read her e-mail faithfully?

Relationships—and team successes—rise and on fall on such issues. So know your teammates' technological tolerance levels. And if someone you must communicate with doesn't like e-mail— call her on the phone.

Remember that e-mail is not the mission—it is merely a means to achieving the mission.

Laurel and Hardy Technologies

Technology can be a blessing or it can, if relied on too heavily, become a dangerous trap. Not long ago we received this e-mail description of a team blinded by technology:

"Our teams have retreated into an e-mail world. We're not sure we can coax them out of the electronic burrow and back to face-to-face communicating. People sitting ten feet apart are writing notes to one another and then routing them through Bolivia."

We are passing through a phase right now of intoxication with networked communications. While we play, and until the fascination fades, onsite team communication is going to suffer. Teams in thrall to their network never have the fresh, synergistic feeling of really working together in real time. Their communications will be static and cold because of the turn-taking that is part of today's posting technologies. Like Laurel and Hardy passing through a doorway, they bog down taking turns.

One solution is to move the furniture around—to reengineer the workplace so that teaming comes naturally. If it seems legitimate to talk to the fellow down the hall by way of Bolivia, put everyone in one big room together. Dismantle the partitions. Some groups need to really live together to become a team. But be careful with togetherness; a little goes a long way.

Another enlivener is a virtual chalkboard. Every system has a network window, on which anyone can scrawl a group message—a deadline, a cartoon, a cherished saying, a reminder. The window is always present in iconized form, and can be zapped to full size with an ALT-SHIFT combination. It is an electronic commons, on which anyone can tell everyone anything.

Before you build the perfect gilded cage for your team, however, remember that only conventional work teams occupy a single space. Most of the teams we are all on are short-term, ad-hoc teams. If your team is the local PTA, that is a team which should not live together.

We know a product development team that is headquartered locally, but with half of its members scattered from heck to breakfast. Three designers are at divisional headquarters here. Four more are employees of four different corporate partners: one is a manufacturer's rep in Columbus; two are production subcontractors in Mexico City and the Philippines; the fourth is a semiretired engineer/telecommuter in Ketchikan, Idaho. The team also claims, as adjunct members, another engineer in Paris, an industrial sales whiz in New York, and the team's corporate sponsor in Osaka.

This is what teams are coming to, and the technologies go way beyond the PC. The Minnesota group formally videoconferences with other members once a week. Because of time zone differences, members draw straws to see who has to face the camera in the middle of the night.

Videoconferencing used to be a big deal—everyone had to go to a private TV studio in the company telecommunications center. Today it's a lot easier—they all have little video eyes mounted in the corners of their PCs. The image is a little stiff and it flickers a bit, but they can now call one another at the drop of a hat and have a conversation with live video of one another on their computer screens. With the advent of broadband transmission, even the flicker is disappearing.

If that sounds extravagant, realize that this is the closest these people ever get to one another. Seeing one another's faces makes everyone seem less Darth Vaderesque. Having real faces to connect with names and voices helped break the ice and helped team formation.

Besides video, the team makes hourly use of fax. This is especially useful to the people in Paris and Japan, who like to not be conscious when the Minnesota members are. Faxing helps them stay current with one another, within a few hours.

Online services are also important. The Japan office subscribes to MCI Mail. Columbus is on America Online. Minneapolis and Japan are hooked up to The Microsoft Network. The fellow in Idaho uses a wireless fax modem with his laptop up at his cabin in the mountains, and it connects with a mom-and-pop Internet gateway in Coeur d'Alene. Using this motley assortment of online providers, the ten team members can send one another daily memos on problems they are facing, and edit versions of one another's documents.

The headquarters half of the team is the envy of the others because they enjoy broadband Internet transmission. But the engineer in Idaho has the sweetest technology: a wireless handheld that can swap e-mail from his cabin atop a blue mountain. Remarkable freedom, with no strings attached.

What's remarkable to us about this team is that it is really doing all this right now. And the team isn't anything exotic—it designs construction crew safety equipment.

We asked one of the team, Kathy, whether her fellow team members felt that the technology was too much, whether they were in danger of vanishing into it and never coming out, like the e-mail moles back in the second paragraph.

"No, we all enjoy it," she said, "because you can see everything. It makes things that are happening very far away seem real, and close by."

Bottom line: a team is still a team, no matter how much hardware and software it drags behind it.

A computer will not impose clarity on a fuzzy notion, or vice versa. That is something only we can do.

If your globally networked team is in trouble from too much technology, here's what you do: Make a point, maybe twice a year, of buying plane tickets and flying to some agreed-upon location, and get to know one another again, in the flesh.

Bring a swimsuit, and make it a vacation.

chapter 31

Long-Term Team Health

And so we draw near the end of the team journey. We've identified all the problems, confusions, and misconceptions that have been keeping teams from performing, and taken steps to get them working the way they should. And you've kicked out the jams. Your group is a lean, mean teaming machine.

But the team journey doesn't end here. Having attained a solid groove, you need to find ways to keep the team there, and to keep the groove from deteriorating into a rut. You want your team to stay hungry and in the chase—even if it has already experienced solid success, even if it is being rewarded and recognized the way it deserves to be.

Sports cliché alert: As hard as it is to win once, it's tons harder to keep winning, year in and year out.

Continuous Clarity

How does a team survive success? By striving to maintain the same level of attention to its own processes that it maintained while it was first achieving success. The point of reference is continuous improvement, what the Japanese call *kaizen*—the idea that processes can be improved infinitely.

Continuous improvement is the way teams should think about how their outputs are received by external groups—end customers, internal customers, other teams, the enterprise as a whole.

For internal purposes, we propose a parallel practice called *continuous clarity*—a never-relax attitude toward resurfacing team dynamics, checking in on and honoring one another's needs and wishes, refocusing on being the best team you can be.

The reason for continuous clarity is that things change. The conditions that existed six months ago, as the team was enjoying obvious success, have given way to new conditions—of the marketplace, of the organization, of the team itself.

The danger is that, as conditions change, the team slips out of congruency with itself. If team business is riding a roller coaster, then you want your team in the same train of cars, and on the same track.

Continuous clarity—bear with this Zen riddle—means you are *constantly reclarifying the clarity you first achieved* during the team's inception. It's the reason why a published "mission statement" loses power over time. The memory of what it means is in constant decay.

Teams need to refresh their vision with new reasons, new perspectives, and deeper convictions. They have to do it today, and tomorrow, and the next day after that.

They need to obtain ongoing clarity on:

▶ high-priority goals with associated short-term tasks;

▶ accountabilities (who's responsible, for what, by when);

▶ barriers and strategies around the barriers;

▶ any interpersonal issues needing addressing;

▶ any needed modifications of leadership strategy; and

▶ suggestions for improving interteam and intrateam communications.

Continuous clarity means continually enumerating the things that lead to team success, and asking if they are working, or if they need work.

We ask if we have the resources we need. If not, where can we get them? And if we can't get them, how do we make do without them?

We think of the people adjuncts that are indispensable to team survival:

▶ *The team sponsor.* This is our team angel, the person who runs interference for us. Is he or she apprised of our current doings, our problems, our needs? What does he or she need to know to continue saving our bacon?

▶ *The team champions.* The individual or individuals high up in the organization whose idea we were, and who helped get us going. Are channels to these persons open? Are they still our friends? Are they still there? What do they need to know to continue serving us? What do we need to know?

▶ *The facilitator.* The outside mediator, whether outside the team or outside the enterprise. This person has the objective eyes to help us see what we cannot see. Are we in touch? What does he or she think?

▶ *Team leaders.* Are the nominal team leaders and the de facto team leaders in synch with the team? What issues do they see coming down the pike? Are they having problems that they haven't informed the rest of the team about?

Without this continuous reclarification, the vision decays and the team, despite absolutely tip-top intentions, breaks up. Some team members may still be on the roller coaster track, but others have diverged and are happily tooling in disconnected coaster cars down Hollywood Boulevard, the Appian Way, or some lonely dirt road way up in the Adirondacks. And that's bad. Interesting, but bad.

Continuous clarity means that a team must adopt an ongoing diagnostic attitude about itself. Remember the grid at the beginning of the book, on page 13, showing the ways that teams go bad, and proposed solutions? As a reader of this book you glanced at it once; you probably thought something like, Eureka!

As a team member committed to maintaining continuous clarity on team excellence, however, you should have a copy of that grid more or less stapled to your mind. Because you need to be thinking all the time about the various ways in which teams get stuck— in order to prevent getting stuck, or to detect getting stuck as early as possible, so as to get quickly unstuck.

The new grid lists the pitfalls teams are prone to, then three measures:

▶ **Where We Were a Year Ago** (on a scale from 1 to 7, with 1 being "rotten" and 7 being "outstanding");

▶ **Where We Are Now** (1–7); and

▶ **Where We Want to Be a Year from Now** (1–7).

A final column allows space for **Action Plan Notes: What We Will Do to Get There.**

When in doubt about your team's current condition of alertness, the grid can serve as a five-minute diagnostic course to identify where problems are occurring and where targeted goals are not being met, and move teams to plan remedies.

By using this grid, or one of your own that lists problems your particular team is prone to, you can maintain a diagnostic attitude that keeps your team from slipping too far from its intended path.

Diagnostic Dangers

Having said what we just said, we feel the need to offer a proviso:

It is good for teams to cultivate a diagnostic attitude, to maintain this continuous clarity.

But it is bad to fall in love with the idea.

PROBLEM	Where We Were a Year Ago	Where We Are Now	Where We Want to Be a Year from Now	Action Plan Notes: What We Will Do to Get There
Mismatched Needs				
Confused Goals, Cluttered Objectives				
Unresolved Roles				
Bad Decision Making				
Uncertain Boundaries				
Bad Policies, Stupid Procedures				
Personality Conflicts				
Bad Leadership				
Bleary Vision				
Anti-Team Culture				
Insufficient Feedback and Information				
Ill-Conceived Reward Systems				
Lack of Team Trust				
Unwillingness to Change				

Usually there is someone on the team who has a knack for the kind of circumspect, see-around-corners thinking that ongoing diagnosis requires. This person is wired a bit differently from most people. He or she may be a bit of a worrier, but quite good at seeing the big picture, and identifying minute variations of team behavior that are leading it astray.

Some teams don't have anyone matching this description. They aren't able to designate anyone as the clarity controller, and they have a dickens of a time staying focused.

Other teams have the opposite problem—one or more members infatuated with the task of diagnosis. They are blessed with the ability to see where the group is slipping off the tracks, and that blessing becomes a curse. They go around all day spotting discrepancies, crying *aha!,* and generally confusing the team worse than it was confusing itself.

We call it diagnostic overload. It happens when the call to clarity itself becomes a distraction. You hear it as one of the wilder aphorisms of the TQM movement, like "If it ain't broke, break it," or "Don't put a fire out when you can prevent it in the first place."

These people are too in love with clarity. Their ego and self-esteem are too bound up in detecting minute variations. They envision the effective team as a crackling synaptic whip of self-correcting maniacs. A pleasant idea, but the reality is that fires are a part of most of our jobs, and when we are on fire, it makes sense to put it out, not pause for a lyrical meditation on the beauty of prevention.

Making a cult of clarification was one of the things teams were implemented to avoid. Teams, you will recall, replaced a system of multilayered controls—other people whose sole job was to keep an eye on you. Let's not do that again.

Epilogue:
Toward Team Intelligence

e began by pledging this wasn't going to be another team happy-talk book. We hope we didn't come across as too negative, though. We believe in teams. But teams are trouble, because they're made of people, and people are trouble.

The happy-talk books pretended that just murmuring the mantra of teams would cause all the creepy organizational goblins—inefficiency, low productivity, befuddled processes, high cost, bloated workforce, poor morale, poor return on investment—to fly away.

Teams would magically outperform the old hierarchical system, and everybody would get along, and you wouldn't need the metal detector at shareholders meetings. Quality without tears.

But hey, guess what: There ain't no such thing as quality, or any kind of organizational transformation, without tears. In fact, tears—meaning, sincerity, commitment, and caring about the people you work with—are probably the best sign you'll get that you're on the right track.

We talked for so many years about "the bottom line," meaning quarterly profits, that we have trouble admitting that there are multiple bottom lines to what we do. Besides lying awake at night worrying about return on outlays, team leaders worry about:

▶ whether leadership is leading;

▶ whether the team "gets" the organizational vision, or its own goals;

▶ whether the full knowledge and intelligence of every team member is being tapped; and

▶ whether the people who make up the team are getting their non-team needs met.

These are not concerns that business schools teach. And yet, in the brave new world of teams materializing around us, they are the concerns that will keep the heart of the modern organization pumping blood.

Team members don't have to be best friends to be a good team. Every team has people who would not pick one another to affiliate with in a thousand millenniums.

But we're not lovers, or even best friends—we're a team. All we have to do is take one another's side on the main issues, doing the job the team exists to do.

Philosopher Terry Warner talks about a "principle of agency," by which all team members become agents for one another, charged with the task of making one another's dreams come true.

A better analogy than friends is family. Like members of a family, team members do not generally ask to be thrown together. Like families, all teams are flawed. Like families, teams have their high points and their low points. Fights break out. Emotions flare.

And just as families usually pool together in a crisis, setting their misgivings aside, so must teams. After all, we spend as much or more time with our teams as we do with our families. And the dreams of our real families often are bound up in the aspirations of the teams we belong to.

In the best teams you see a circle—of sympathy, support, and a limited kind of love. It is the love engendered when team members sincerely want the best for one another.

In good teams, you see at the very least an ongoing curiosity about one another. How can we be so different and still work together? How do we harness the power of our differentness? What must we do to continue to share information and create new knowledge? Curiosity, the key to our own intelligence, likely is the key to team intelligence.

If the team movement arose from any single ethic, it was that people are not cogs and levers, as the old organizational diagrams suggested. We are human beings. Ignore the interior workings, the strivings and desires, and team failure is inevitable.

But when people take the time to learn about one another, what is in their hearts as well as in their minds, we rise to a higher level.

Call it love, call it curiosity, call it team intelligence, or don't call it anything at all.

But somehow or other, you have to get there. It is the glory of working together, and getting things right.

Index

About the Authors

Harvey Robbins discovered the joy of teaming at age 8 when he was picked up by police in the Tremont section of the Bronx for gang activities—rock throwing and fighting. He was a member of the same gang his mother had belonged to a generation before, and belonging taught him some of the basic precepts of what kinds of groups flourish, and what kinds never will.

This curious turn continued in college, where he was a nationally ranked sharpshooter, and was recruited by intelligence agencies. Fortunately for somebody, he discovered psychology, and his focus took a 180-degree turn toward issues of organizational dysfunction, and how to avoid and repair them. The two halves of his life came together in his 1988 book *Turf Wars,* in which he likened work team problems to the mindsets of embattled street gangs.

The follow-up to *Turf Wars, Why Teams Don't Work,* written with Michael Finley, won the 1995 Financial Times/Booz Allen & Hamilton Global Business Book Award for best management book published in the Americas.

He is also author or co-author of numerous other books, including *How to Speak and Listen Effectively, Why Change Doesn't Work,* and *Transcompetition.* He is currently embarked on a book project on the subject of leadership.

Harvey holds a doctorate in clinical psychology from Texas A&M—Commerce. His consulting topics include team development, change management, competition vs. collaboration (transcompetition), organization and leadership effectiveness, and interpersonal influence.

Clients of his firm Robbins & Robbins include American Express, AT&T, Allied Signal, FMC, General Dynamics, Honeywell, 3M, International Multifoods, Johnson & Johnson, Southern Company, Target Stores, Toro, US West, the U.S. Secret Service, U.S. Customs, and the Internal Revue Service.

Harvey, wife and fellow psychologist Nancy, and son Max live in Minnetonka, Minnesota.

Harvey A. Robbins
Robbins & Robbins
2475 Ridgewater Drive
Minnetonka, MN 55343
612-544-9260
e-mail: robbi004@maroon.tc.umn.edu
URL: www.harveyrobbins.com

Michael Finley was a general-purpose journalist until he watched 4,000 people line up in the ice and snow for 20 jobs at an automotive supplier in rust-belt Milwaukee in 1983. It was a heartbreaking scene, and it impressed upon him the plight of the worker in a rapidly changing society. Since then, change, technology, and the development of peoplecentric organizations has been the focus of much of his writing.

In 1998 Mike was named one of a score of "Wizards of the Wired World" by *Financial Times Press*, along with Arthur C. Clarke, Alvin Toffler, Nicholas Negroponte, and others. He is a regular panelist on the Peabody-nominated PBS program "Mental Engineering," and head writer for The Masters Forum in Minneapolis.

Mike writes a weekly e-letter about change called "Future Shoes." Besides being distributed by e-mail, these letters appear regularly in *Computer User*, the *San Francisco Examiner*, the Albany *Times Union*, and other publications. Mike's work has appeared in publications as wide-ranging as *Rolling Stone*, *Paris Review*, and *Across the Board*.

Mike lives in St. Paul with his wife Rachel, daughter Daniele, son Jon, and a poodle dog.

Mike makes his electronic abode at www.mfinley.com, which he loves more than anything except his wife, daughter, son, and maybe poodle.

Michael Finley
1841 Dayton Avenue
St. Paul, MN 55104
651-644-4540
fax: 651-644-5226
e-mail: mfinley@mfinley.com
URL: www.mfinley.com